Social Work and the Sociology of Organizations

W9-AFF-560

LIBRARY OF SOCIAL WORK

GENERAL EDITOR:—NOEL TIMMS

*Professor of Applied Social Studies,
University of Bradford*

Social Work and the Sociology of Organizations

by Gilbert Smith

Research Fellow in Sociology
University of Aberdeen

LONDON
ROUTLEDGE & KEGAN PAUL

First published 1970
by Routledge & Kegan Paul Ltd
Broadway House, 68-74 Carter Lane
London, E.C.4
Printed in Great Britain
by Northumberland Press Limited
Gateshead
ISBN 0 7100 6873 5 (c)
ISBN 0 7100 6874 3 (p)

General editor's introduction

The Library of Social Work is designed to meet the needs of students following courses of training for social work. In recent years the number and kinds of training in Britain have increased in an unprecedented way. But there has been no corresponding increase in the supply of textbooks to cover the growing differentiation of subject matter or to respond to the growing spirit of enthusiastic but critical enquiry into the range of subjects relevant to social work. The Library will consist of short texts designed to introduce the student to the main features of each topic of enquiry, to the significant theoretical contributions so far made to its understanding, and to some of the outstanding problems. Each volume will suggest ways in which the student might continue his work by further reading.

As the author points out, organizations have been categorized and compared in many different ways. They have been described in terms of their prime beneficiary or in terms of the goals they pursue, but, as Gilbert Smith amply illustrates, no single category can catch and hold the full complexity of organizational life. His demonstration of the losses and gains incurred through the use of the main concepts so far developed in this field of study is a welcome antidote to the tendency amongst social workers to espouse particular approaches in a rather wholesale manner. The first part of this book outlines and discusses the main concepts of goals, compliance, bureaucracy, front-line organization, the total institution, and the permeable organization. In the second part of the book the author considers a selected number of specific organizations, using the framework of concepts established in the first section. The organizations studied constitute

a helpfully wide range, including both social work organizations and others such as hospitals and schools.

Social workers are now beginning to show considerable curiosity about the organizations in which they work or with which their clients are closely associated. They see in general that the organization is not to be regarded as a container for precious social work methodologies or as simply a grossly distorting bureaucratic pressure, but the subtle and pervasive interplay between social work activities and the organization to which they 'belong' requires careful and detailed study. It can be approached from a number of different starting points, and each of these has been used in the Library of Social Work. Organizations can be studied as part of the attempt to explore the general contribution of sociology to social work (hence the references in Leonard's *Sociology in Social Work* to bureaucracy and social work organizations). Alternatively, we can approach the subject from the viewpoint of the administrator of the social work agency (as in Wareham's *Introduction to Administration for Social Workers*). Finally, theories of organization can be selected for detailed study and critically discussed from the point of view of their internal consistency and their application to social work organizations. This is the approach of the present volume. It is particularly appropriate at the present time when developments in the organization of the personal social services emphasize the importance of knowledge of organizational factors in the equipment of the social worker of the future, whether or not he or she attains a job with high administrative content. Social workers need to learn as much as they can from theories of organization not in order to receive a perfect plan or a dogma, but so that they can begin to work out the nature of the required 'fit' between organizational structure and the professional tasks of social work.

NOEL TIMMS

Contents

Acknowledgments

A number of people have helped in the preparation of this book. Although the final responsibility is my own, I would like to thank in particular Dennis Marsden, Adrian Sinfield, Jef Smith and J. Graham Smith for comments on early chapters, and Noel Timms for advice throughout.

I completed the final chapters in Aberdeen while working on a research project supported by the Nuffield Provincial Hospitals Trust.

G.S.

Introduction

Although social work thinking and practice has often been concerned with the one-to-one relationship between client and worker, we are now beginning to understand the way in which organizational factors consistently intervene. In studies of role, reference group, social policy and social change, in the sociology of the family and in urban community studies, sociology is making a number of important contributions to social work. But since most social work takes place within the context of an organization, one field of sociology which is especially useful to the social worker is that of the sociology of organizations. Indeed one writer (Meyer, 1968, p. 156) has gone so far as to claim that, 'The utility of sociological analysis to social work is nowhere more evident than at the organizational level.'

With the broadening of the sociology of organizations from early studies of industry and then government, to welfare agencies, prisons, mental hospitals, probation offices, residential homes and voluntary service organizations, with the publication of the Seebohm report (1968) on the personal social services in England and Wales, and with the establishment of new social work departments in Scotland, particular attention has been focused on the organizational context of social work practice.

What happens when bureaucratic and professional norms conflict? How does a voluntary organization differ from a statutory agency? How does the communication structure of a Children's Department influence case-work practice? What are the results of the conflicting demands of 'custody' and 'treatment' goals? These are the sort of questions we need to answer.

Type of organization

Numerous distinctions have been employed to describe and compare organizations. They have been labelled bureaucratic or non-bureaucratic, democratic or oligarchic, as processing people or processing things, as normative, utilitarian or coercive. In describing social work organiza-tions one scheme has been used more than most: Blau and Scott's (1963) division based on 'prime beneficiary' (see, for example, Eyden, 1969).

Here organizations are classified on the basis of *cui bono*: who benefits. 'Mutual benefit' associations primarily benefit the members, 'business concerns' the owners, 'ser-vice organizations' the clients, and 'common-weal organiza-tions' the public at large. This scheme is then used to show that particular problems are associated with each type of organization. The central problem in mutual benefit associations is said to be that of maintaining the internal democratic process; in business concerns, that of maximiz-ing operative efficiency; in service organizations, that of reconciling professional service with administrative pro-cess; and in common-weal organizations, that of develop-ing democratic external control of the organization by the public. In the terms of this division, social work organizations are generally termed 'service organizations'.

However, when we come to classify any particular organization we find that the task is by no means as simple as at first appears. For example, Blau himself (1963) in a study of a law enforcement agency, which is appar-ently defined as a common-weal organization, describes the agents as seeing themselves as professionals offering a service to their clients. They refused to bring charges against businessmen who offered them bribes because they defined their agency as a service organization. A social work agency is classed by Blau and Scott as a service organization, yet a probationer, or family faced with a court order placing their child in care, might well view it as an instrument of social control—a common-weal organization. Prisons *are* described as common-weal organizations, yet one principle of prison re-organization is rehabilitation and reform—quite as much a service to clients as casework practice in an agency. And, to take a final example, what is an old people's home? It is generally thought to benefit the clients. But there is a sense in which it is common-weal in removing from society those who can no longer perform their expected roles. And for those homes which are privately run it also benefits the owners in making a financial profit. Blau and Scott agree, it is true, that, 'the prime beneficiary is not the only beneficiary', but we are given no way of telling which beneficiary is prime.

Neither do all the empirical studies we have confirm Blau and Scott's hypotheses about the crucial problems faced by each type of organization. Labour Unions, classed as mutual benefit associations, face, we are told, the problem of maintaining democratic control. But in their study of the International Typographical Union, Lispet, Trow and Coleman (1956) show that given certain patterns of communication, association and career structure, democratic control need be no problem at all. Again, we are told that the main problem for common-weal organizations is that of external control. Yet studies of mental hospitals and prisons repeatedly state as their central concern the tension resulting from conflicting demands of custody and reform.

There are three basic reasons for this confusion. First, the propositions about crucial problems faced by each type of organization are not empirically based but are derived from the original classification. It is assumed that the most important problem faced by the organization will be that problem which is of greatest concern to the 'prime beneficiary'. The central problem of a prison is thought to be that of external democratic control because that is the problem which is of greatest concern to the general public. The problem I have already mentioned, the conflicting demands of custody and reform, is primarily a problem for the prison staff. Blau and Scott identify the interests of the organization as a whole with those of only one group, and this neglects the interests of other groups as they attempt to pursue them.

Second, there is no way of measuring the relative benefits (and it is a measurement problem) as a basis for judging which beneficiary is prime. Since each party may benefit in a very different way the benefits cannot be directly compared on a single, even ordinal scale. How can we relate, say, the salary of a social worker with the benefits accruing to a child who is successfully placed for adoption?

Third, the function of an organization in society (see Leonard, 1966, p. 25) is confused (1) with the formal ideology of the organization and (2) with its policy in operation. These are all independent and there may be conflicts between them. Indeed it is only by understanding these conflicts that we can understand some of the most important features of an organization's structure.

Thus, the claim that all social work organizations can be classed as service organizations is an oversimplification which confuses as much as it clarifies. It may be an accurate description of the formal ideology. We are not so much concerned with this ideal picture. We are more concerned with the real constraints of organizational structure in that loose grouping of organizations with which social workers are most likely to be concerned—social work agencies and institutions, voluntary service organizations, hospitals, prisons and schools.

Type of study

There are several possible approaches to the study of
social work organizations. First, a study may focus
primarily upon the place of the organization within its
external environment, or upon the internal structure of
the organization itself. Second, the method of investigation may be normative in setting out prescriptive statements of what 'should' be done, or it may simply be
explanatory in formulating and testing particular hypotheses in order to arrive at a fuller understanding of the
way the organization functions. These four possible
different approaches are set out in Table 1.

Table 1

Method of Investigation

Primary Focus	*Prescriptive*	*Explanatory*
	I	II
External Environment (macro studies)	Social Policy Formulation	Studies of the Outcome of Social Policy
	III	IV
Internal Structure (micro studies)	Principles of Social Service Administration	The Sociology of Social Work Organizations

(Adapted from Zaleznick and Jardian,
1967)

This book is mainly concerned with the fourth type of
study; explanatory studies of the internal structure of
social work and related organizations. So this is not a
book which sets out in 'blueprint' the most 'efficient'
structures for social work organization. It takes existing
organizations as they are and examines the limitations
imposed by the organizational setting.

There is one final comment by way of introduction.

The sociology of organizations, the approach adopted here, is devoted to discovering the cause and results of different characteristics of organizations. Organization theory, on the other hand, is basically concerned with improving organizational efficiency through principles of administration. But the two are clearly related and each must understand the other. As Albrow (1968, p. 166) points out, 'The sociologist must constantly re-examine the relations between practical discourse and his own language of analysis' while, 'The organization theorist (and, I would add, the social worker) is bound to take cognizance of any contribution to knowledge about organizations.'

Part One:

The nature of organizations

1
Goals of the organization

The concept 'organizational goal' is central in the socio-logical study of organizations. Indeed, many writers employ it as the major defining characteristic. For Blau and Scott (1963, p. 1) an organization is 'a social unit ... that has been established for the explicit purpose of achieving certain goals'; for Talcott Parsons (1960, p. 17) 'As a formal analytical point of reference, primacy of orientation to the attainment of a specific goal is used as the defining characteristic of an organization which distinguishes it from other types of social system', and for Etzioni (1961, p. 79) 'organizations are social units oriented to the realization of specific goals'.

The goal concept is thus the central feature of the model upon which much of the writing and research about organizations is based. This model is implicit, for example, in the concept of 'the primary task' (Rice, 1963), a notion that is used a good deal within social work. It has been variously called the 'rational model' (Gouldner, 1959), the 'goal model' (Etzioni, 1960), and the 'orthodox model' (Albrow, 1968). In giving a brief outline of the model I shall use Albrow's term.

The orthodox model

A goal is the image of a desired future state which may or may not be brought about. The organizational goal is the state of affairs which the organization is attempting to realize. Organizations are thus seen as 'instruments': rationally conceived means to the realization of a single, specific, stable and generally accepted group goal.

In order to achieve this, organizations have a formally defined structure laid down in written rules and regulations. There is a rigid hierarchy of control and an extensive division of labour in which each member of the organization has a prescribed task. The existence of the organization is explained in terms of its goal and because they are thus formally established for an explicit purpose, organizations, more than other social groups, are thought to be in control of their nature and development. To quote Etzioni:

> They (organizations) are planned, deliberately structured, constantly and self consciously reviewing their performances, and restructuring themselves accordingly. In this sense organizations are unlike natural social units, such as the family, ethnic group or community. (1965, p. 650)

At first this seems a good enough model to employ. In a Probation Department, for example, we can find in written statements (legislation, recruiting publicity, etc.) the goal of the organization. The hierarchy of control is clear, from the Principal Probation Officer downwards. It is through this hierarchy that the work of the department is controlled; caseloads set, court work arranged, consultations given and other duties performed. Detailed rules and regulations can be found in written Home Office circulars, contracts of employment and the like. If change is required, the agency can also change.

But in studying social work organizations we must look at more than the formal 'blueprint' and the organization chart. Does the pattern of control really work in this way? All rules and regulations need interpretation. How does this occur? Are there 'unanticipated consequences' to planned organizational change? How do informal communications affect the agency structure? In recent thinking (much of which owes a good deal to studies of hospitals, prisons, voluntary associations and field work agencies), a number of important criticisms are made of this orthodox model.

The notion of 'organizational goal' is now seen as too simple to deal with the real complex of goals that exist in any organization. The model is value biased. It is over rationalistic. And in studies based on this model there is a basic methodological error.

The complex goals of organizations

(1) Multiple goals

Even in their formal statements most organizations have several goals rather than just one single aim. A Children's Department arranges adoptions, conducts 'preventive' family casework and visits private foster homes as well as looking after children in care. In providing student supervision it may perform a teaching function as well. A university conducts research as well as teaching. Charitable and voluntary organizations are concerned both with the interests of their clients and with the social activities of their members. Religious organizations evangelize, worship and tithe.

Such multiple goals as these, even when complementary, produce conflicts. There are conflicts in allocating resources. In a League of Hospital Friends time spent on organizing a social evening is time lost to visiting patients. Does a university department with a budget surplus devote more funds to research or does it engage an additional teaching member of staff?

There are problems of control. Different decision-making structures may be employed for different goals. Personnel most able to supervise the activities relating to one goal may be least able in the case of another. One set of tasks may require greater autonomy than another. Harrison's study (1959) provides a good example here. The Southern Baptist Convention had to maintain the autonomy of the local church whilst providing a centralized structure for achieving missionary and evangelistic goals. As Harrison comments, 'The tension between these imperative goals has been at the root of the Baptist problem. Important anomalies have been born out of this tension.' (p. 52)

Multiple goals are even more important if the goals themselves conflict. The best example of this is the prison. Many of the requirements of 'custody' and 'reform' are mutually exclusive. This is explored in greater detail in Chapter 9.

(2) *Diffuse goals*
The official goals of an organization are invariably general and vague. Stated at a high level of abstraction they must be translated into operative goals before they can be used as the basis of policy. For example, if the aim of International Voluntary Service, is that of 'furthering international understanding' should it affiliate to CND? At one time or another in recent years, IVS, Oxfam, Shelter, and UNA, have all been divided on political questions. Although different groups within each organization claim to pursue the same general goal, they interpret this in different ways.

One local branch of the 'Haslemere Group' urged local churches to unite. Another studied root crop production in the East Anglican Fens. Both claimed to be putting into practice the overall goals of the movement which were concerned with encouraging the churches to devote more of their resources to alleviating world poverty. In the employment agency studied by Blau (1963) the choice of which goal was implemented in practice depended upon interpretation of the agency rules. The orthodox model fails to see the complexity in this process of operationalization.

(3) *Perceived goals*

When we look beyond formal written statements we encounter another complexity. Not only do members operationalize goals in different ways. They invariably disagree in their perception of these goals.

Peabody (1964), for example, conducted a comparative study of three organizations: a police department, a welfare office, and an elementary school. In none of these did he find consensus in perceptions of the organization's goals. When he asked members of the welfare office to identify two or three of the most important things that the organization should be doing, 83% mentioned client welfare, 35% financial assistance, 26% community service, 22% public relations and 22% co-operation with other agencies. In the Police Department 69% mentioned crime prevention, 57% law enforcement, 45% traffic control, 30% public relations and an information service, and 24% criminal investigation. He found similar disagreement in the school. Parallel findings are reported in studies by Blau (1963), Harrison (1959), and Sills (1957).

(4) *Changing goals*

The goals of an organization are often subject to change. This happens in a number of ways.

The sociologist, Robert Michels, was the first to notice the phenomenon of 'goal displacement' in which a minor goal replaces the existing dominant goal. The most common form of displacement is that in which the procedures designed to administer a goal become the goal itself. This is most usually associated with bureaucratic organizations. In one employment agency in which statistical records were used to record performance, workers

7

adopted procedures which improved their monthly ratings but caused inconvenience to clients seeking employment (Blau, 1963).

The 'succession of goals' in an organization is another way in which they can change. This occurs if the goals are achieved or become irrelevant in a changed environment. The Birth Control Federation in America, for example, now offers treatment for fertility and sex education. The succession of goals is a particular feature of voluntary organizations.

Value bias in the orthodox model

In a recent article Martin Albrow (1968) explains that mistakes have been made because the orthodox model is biased in its values. In paying so much attention to the achievement of specific goals the model identifies the organization with the interests of only one group. He argues that the orthodox model does not present a picture of real organizations but only of hypothetical or ideological future situations. And this, he explains, can be dangerous.

> In a situation where the members of an organization themselves disagree as to what constitutes the organizational goal, the requirements of the orthodox definition can severely prejudice an objective account. At its worst, the student's determination to impute clear cut goals can lead him to a point where he is actually siding with one party or another in saying what the objectives ought to be. (p. 155)

In order to avoid this mistake he suggests the following definition of an organization:

> organizations are social units where individuals are conscious of their membership and legitimize their co-operative activities primarily by reference to the attainment of impersonal goals rather than to moral standards. (p. 162)

8

This formulation retains the importance of goal attainment as the distinctive characteristic of organizations but it avoids assuming that goals are either unitary, specific, stable or causally significant. It also avoids regarding goals as the property of any one group. Most important of all, it avoids identifying the research problem with the interests of organizational managers or other 'higher participants'.

The over rationalistic orthodox model

In identifying the organization with only one set of interests the orthodox model is over rationalistic. The managerial élite is seen as using rational and logical means to pursue clearly formulated ends while other members of the organization (the 'lower participants') are governed by a non-rational orientation.

Perrow (1961) insists that this level of analysis is inadequate since it fails to account for the real changes in the goals of an organization. It is not an explanation, he says, to regard changes as simply irrational deviations. We must distinguish between 'official' goals and 'operative' goals, the ends sought through the actual operating policies of the organization. They tell us what the organization is actually trying to do, regardless of what the official goals say they are trying to do.

I will deal with the body of Perrow's paper in Chapter 7, for his comments are based on a study of voluntary general hospitals, but his general conclusions are important at this stage. Every organization, he claims, must accomplish several tasks and a particular group within the organization is associated with the duties of each task. The operative goals of an organization are tied directly to the interests of these groups. To understand the real goals we have to understand the organizational conflicts, for the operative goals of the organization depend upon which is the dominant group at any particular time. Let

9

us take an example of the sort of study Perrow's conclusions lead us to propose.

Impressionistic evidence suggests that in Mental Health services the goals of officers who have recently completed training differ from those who have no professional qualification. (See Seebohm (1968) Appendix M for statistics.) Thus, if Perrow's conclusions are correct we would expect the operative goals of a mental health department to change as newly qualified officers were promoted, in spite of the fact that official goals might remain unchanged throughout.

The orthodox model is also over rationalistic in promoting the 'unhistorical myth' (Albrow, 1968), in which an account of the origin of an organization is given in terms of its goal. In fact examples of organizations with a single, simple purpose and abrupt foundation are extremely rare. Far more typical is the birth of the 'Seebohm departments' amid the conflicting interests of professional social workers and Medical Officers of Health.

Usually the formation of goals is a long and complex process. Residential homes for the aged have their origin in the poor law and the work house. The comprehensive school has its origin in the tripartite system. In the historical study of organizations the analysis of current goals should be the conclusion rather than the starting point of the study. It is an over rationalistic conception of both the nature of man and the nature of organization that sees historical development simply in terms of pursuing the original goal.

Methodology of the orthodox model

In spite of these criticisms the literature based on the orthodox model is full of studies which set out to assess the effectiveness of the organization's goals. These studies usually show that the organization is ineffective and has goals which differ from those that it claims.

Etzioni (1960) argues that these studies have little empirical value because the findings are the result of the way in which the studies are conducted. They commit the basic methodological error of comparing the present state of an organization (a real state) with the organizational goal (an ideal state) as if the goal were real. If we compare the real with the ideal most levels of performance will seem poor.

Etzioni is not saying that the findings of these studies are wrong. He is saying that based as they are on the orthodox model they are inevitable. And findings which are inevitable can never be more than trivial.

One example of a study which makes this mistake is Adrian Sinfield's paper (1969), 'Which Way for Social Work?' Sinfield claims that the goals of social work are rarely clearly stated. If they are, and then used for assessment, performance levels are poor. However, it is not a deficiency (from a value free perspective) of social work organizations that their goals are diffuse. The deficiency is in the orthodox model which erroneously expects them to be specific. Again, it is only the value bias of the orthodox model which chooses formal goals as the standard for assessing performance. It is not that Sinfield's findings are wrong, but they have little empirical value if they can be deduced from the way in which the study is conducted.

Conclusion

In this section I have argued that the orthodox model fails to cope with the real complexity of goals in social work organizations. I have outlined three criticisms which suggest why this is so. The model is value biased, over rationalistic and leads to methodological errors.

In order to understand the complexities we must abandon the simple notion of organizational goal as a defining characteristic. We must adopt models which pay more attention to the interests of different groups within the organization: field workers, clients, bureaucrats, inmates and residential staff. We must look at the way in which these groups define their own interests, pursue their own goals and, through professional training, communication, authority, bureaucratic, charismatic and other controls, implement their own definitions of the situation. A comment by Rhenman (1968) is useful in summary. The concept of organizational goal, he says,

> is most useful if it is linked to some type of perception of the desired consequences of the activities of the organization, as viewed by a member of the organization, or by an outside observer. It is important to state whose goal perception is being considered. (p. 275)

In many other contexts sociologists have explained the social structure by reference to the demands of competing groups. The organizations of social work may be interpreted in a similar way.

2

Compliance in organizations

The comparative study of organizations

Although we can learn a good deal about social work organizations through propositions about the general similarities between organizations, there are clearly important differences between types of organizations. To ignore this is to invite error. Etzioni (1961), for example, quotes the case of a management consultant firm reporting on the organization of the Roman Catholic Church. The main recommendations were quite inappropriate: that the church should maintain depreciation reserves and that the Pope should delegate some of his authority to subordinates. The model used was based upon the study of large business corporations and ignored features which were peculiar to the Church. A recent unpublished report on a British voluntary service organization provides another example. The consultant equated money, labour and need in the voluntary organization with finance, production and sales in industry. As a result of this inappropriate application of an economic model to a voluntary service organization most of the recommendations made were abandoned within nine months. As Etzioni explains:

Policy recommendations based on such a 'universal' model can lead to ill advised action. Consultants work-

> ing with one of the universal models ... tend to recom-
> mend changes designed to bring the organization into
> line with the model. (1961, p. xiii)

In using the sociology of organizations in social work we
must therefore look at systematic differences between different types of organization as well as at the general
characteristics of organizations.

Compliance as a comparative base

Compliance, 'a relationship consisting of the power
employed by superiors to control subordinates and the
orientation of the subordinate to this power' (Etzioni, 1961,
p. xv), is one base for the comparative study of organizations.

In the study of social work organizations this concept
has two important merits. First it avoids a major defect of
the 'orthodox model' by taking into account the interests
of more than just one group in the organization; it considers both the power of superordinates and the involvement of subordinates. Second, it pays attention both to
the social system of the organization (in examining the
distribution of power) and to the personality system (in
examining members' motivation). Perry Levinson (1964)
has particularly developed this aspect in his analysis of
chronic dependency on social welfare in the United States.

Etzioni's typology of compliance relations relates three
kinds of power with three kinds of involvement.

(1) Kinds of power

Power differs according to the means which 'élites' use to
control those of lower rank, the 'lower participants'. There
are three kinds. Coercive power depends upon the use of
threat or physical force. Remunerative power is based on
material rewards such as money. Normative power rests

on the allocation of symbolic reward such as status symbols and marks of esteem and prestige. Etzioni argues that although the élites of organizations employ all three kinds of power, they tend to emphasize only one and rely less on the others. Teachers in progressive schools, for example, tend to oppose corporal punishment. Social workers may use coercive power, backed by the courts, but casework is primarily based on normative control.

(2) *Kinds of involvement*

Etzioni defines involvement thus: 'Involvement refers to the cathectic-evaluative orientation of an actor to an object, characterised in terms of intensity and direction' (1961, p. 9). This means that members of the organization who are relatively low in the hierarchy may feel indifferent about the way in which 'élites' exercise their powers or they may react strongly. They may also approve or they may disapprove. Alienative involvement is strong disapproval. Calculative involvement is relative indifference, dependent upon the remunerative rewards obtained. Moral involvement is strong approval. Respective examples are given of prisoners of war, trading merchants, and church parishioners.

(3) *A typology of compliance relations*

A compliance relation involves both the type of power applied to a participant in the organization and the type of involvement felt by the participant. In any organization Etzioni suggests that one type of compliance relation predominates. There are thus nine possible types of organization. These are set out in Table 2 (Etzioni 1961 p. 12).

Table 2

A typology of organizations by compliance relation

Kinds of Power   Kinds of Involvement

	Alienative	Calculative	Moral
Coercive	1. (Coercive)	2.	3.
Remunerative	4.	5. (Utilitarian)	6.
Normative	7.	8.	9. (Normative)

Although all nine types are possible, Etzioni claims that three (types 1, 5, 9) are in practice found more than the others since they are more effective. There is a general tendency for organizations to assume one of these three forms. The frequently quoted three-fold typology of organizations (coercive, utilitarian, normative) is thus not a complete typology of organizations but only of the three 'congruent' types.

(4) *A correlate of compliance: goals*

Organizational goals are divided into three types: order, economic, and cultural. Organizations with order goals attempt to control those who are deviant in a society. Those with economic goals produce goods and services. Those with cultural goals attempt to create and preserve 'symbolic objects'. This last is a wide category and includes research organizations which 'create' new culture, churches which reinforce existing culture, and therapeutic mental hospitals which are said to reinforce in their patients a commitment to certain norms and beliefs. The relationship between compliance and goals is summarized in two statements. (1) 'Organizations that have similar compliance structures tend to have similar goals.' (2) 'Certain combinations of compliance and goals are more effective than others.' The relationship is set out in Table 3 (Etzioni 1961 p. 74).

Table 3

Goals and compliance

Types of organization   *Organizational goals*
(Compliance structures)

	Order	Economic	Culture
Coercive	1.	2.	3.
Utilitarian	4.	5.	6.
Normative	7.	8.	9.

Again all nine types are possible but there is a predicted tendency to types 1, 5, 9, because these are seen as the most efficient.

Classification on the basis of compliance

Typical coercive organizations are concentration camps, prisoner-of-war camps, prisons, traditional 'correctional institutions', and custodial mental hospitals. With the exception of some highly professionalized groups, industrial organizations are utilitarian. The category of normative organizations includes religious organizations such as churches and monasteries, political organizations, hospitals, therapeutic mental hospitals, universities, schools and voluntary associations. It has been generally assumed that social work organizations are normative organizations. It is certainly alien to the ideology of social work to consider either physical force or financial inducement as a part of the control structure.

However, attempts to use this typology in research have shown that it is not always easy to classify a particular social work organization. Let us take as an example a major social work agency such as a welfare department. Etzioni refers to 'a social work agency', an American

Welfare Department, as a professional organization (p. 133) and professional organizations are normative (p. 41). In normative organizations 'lower participants' have moral involvement (p. 12). The 'lower participants' of a welfare department, however, are referred to as 'clients', yet in another place (p. 17) Etzioni says that, 'Clients designates people with alienative or calculative involvement.' There are several underlying reasons for this confusion.

Confusion in the notion of compliance

(1) Formal ideology and operative policy

I have already pointed to the difference between the formal ideology of an organization and its operative policy. The typology of compliance relations confuses these, for the kinds of power are those of the formal ideology, whereas the kinds of involvement may be those of the formal ideology or they may be those in operation. Thus, it is not always clear whether statements are being made about the ideology of the organization or about organizational behaviour.

(2) 'Effectiveness'

The notion of 'effectiveness' is confused. In the typology of compliance relations we are told that the congruent case of, for example, coercive power and alienative involvement (coercive compliance), is found so often because it is effective in terms of the goals (presumably formal) of the organization. But it is only effective in terms of the goals if these are order goals. A prison is certainly not effective in terms of the economic goals of producing goods. Before we can accept the basic assumption that 'organizations are social units under pressure ... to be effective' (p. 13) we have to assume that coercive organizations do in fact have order goals. But in the later typology of goals and compliance the relation between coercive organizations and order goals is stated as an empirical finding. The argument is circular. The claims to an empirical finding at the end of the argument are in fact built in as an assumption at the start.

(3) *Organizational goals*

Use of the idea of organizational goal is confusing. In fact the term is used to mean the goals of higher participants and as I have already argued there is little evidence to confirm the assumption that lower participants will share this definition. And lower participants will adopt those kinds of involvement most appropriate to the goals as they see them.

(4) *A two class model*

The dichotomy between 'higher' and 'lower' participants also involves a misleading assumption. A two class model is assumed. Many organizations, it is true, do have an apparent 'status schism' (but see Sykes (1961) on this point). There is a fundamental distinction between staff and children in a children's home, between teachers and pupils in a school, between warders and inmates in a prison, between staff and members of a voluntary organization, between social workers and agency clients. But an organization is not just a simple 'dyadic' relation. We have to consider relations within the major groups in the organizational hierarchy. The relations between a headmaster and his staff will affect the relations between teachers and pupils. The relation between a Director of Social Work and his staff will affect relations between social workers and clients. A 'lower participant' in one relation may thus be a 'higher participant' in another. It seems unlikely that any one type of compliance relation will characterize all relations within an organization.

(5) *Incongruent types and social order*

Etzioni largely ignores structural conflict. He is concerned with social order. Compliance is 'the organizational equivalent of social order' (p. xvii); as he explains in his introduction, 'Broadly interpreted, the study of compliance may contribute to the study of social order' (p. xv). In the text of 313 pages only thirteen lines are devoted to the nine incongruent types.

This leads to error. The prison, for example, is classed as a coercive organization. But Gresham Sykes (1961) has shown that the social structure of a prison is such that the guard must often abandon the coercive basis of his power, and adopt a remunerative basis:

> A guard cannot rely on the direct application of force to achieve compliance, for he is one man against hundreds ... A guard cannot easily rely on threats of punishment, for he is dealing with men who are already being punished near the limits permitted by society ... One of the best 'offers' he can make is ignoring minor offences or making sure that he never places himself in a position to discover infractions of the rules. (pp. 194-5)

This is the sort of data that is difficult to explain if we limit our theory only to the congruent types and to the study of social order.

In these criticisms I have highlighted those aspects of organizations in which there is tension, conflict and change. None of these comments is meant to imply that we should abandon the concept of compliance. But they do imply that in social work, incongruent types of compliance relation are quite as important as congruent types for a complete understanding of the organization.

An incongruent type of compliance

Many welfare agencies have clients, both individuals and families, who have relied upon the agency, continuously or intermittently, for a very long time. The position of the 'chronically dependent' client is clarified if we view the organizational context in terms of its compliance relations.

Typically, chronic dependency is described within a psychological framework. The client is seen as disabled (perhaps from childhood experiences) in his dependency needs. Casework practice is based on the assumption of a normative compliance relation. However, there may be a lack of congruence between the agency's use of normative power and the client's involvement (Levinson 1964). 'Chronic dependency' is a generic term for persistent involvement with an agency, and this can include calculative and alienative involvement, as well as moral. Clients are particularly likely to have a calculative orientation towards receiving relief. Apparently 'inadequate' mothers, for example, may suddenly want their children at home as the children approach school leaving age and can thus support themselves. (For a case study see Norman, 1969.) Clients may even approach several agencies in the hope of increasing their benefits.

If it is assumed that in the welfare agency compliance relations are congruent and normative, tension and conflict appear to derive from the psychological state of the client. In fact the relation may be an incongruent type of compliance (either type 7 or 8 in Table 2). Many of the conflicts involved in dealing with 'chronic dependents' actually derive from the organizational structure of the agency itself. These conflicts are enhanced if the social workers involved fail to understand the incongruent nature of the structure of their organization.

Conclusion

In this section I have outlined a typology of organizations based on the type of compliance relation. The assumption that organizations tend to one of three 'congruent' types is criticized. In social work the typology is as useful in describing the 'incongruent' types as the 'congruent' types of compliance. The analysis of chronic dependency on welfare services is one example of the way in which the concept of compliance can be used in social work to highlight tension and conflict as it occurs at the organizational level.

3
Bureaucracy

The term 'bureaucracy' is so widely used in the study of organizations that at times it seems to be a synonym for organization itself. This is misleading for, stripped of its perjorative connotations, bureaucracy is a particular form of organizational structure, first studied systematically by Max Weber. There are numerous summaries of and commentaries on Weber's theory of bureaucracy (Gerth and Mills, 1948, Blau 1956, Thompson 1961, Etzioni 1964, Mouzelis 1967, and in this series Leonard 1966 and Wareham 1967), but stated briefly, the main characteristics of the bureaucratic type of organization are:

(1) A hierarchical authority structure based on official position rather than the individuality of the incumbent.
(2) A system of rules governing the rights and duties of these positions.
(3) A detailed system of rules and regulations for dealing with each particular case.
(4) A clear-cut and highly specialized division of labour.
(5) Impersonal social relations, with management based on written documents (the 'files').
(6) Recruitment of officials to a salaried career with security of tenure on the basis of technical qualifications.

Weber's major conclusions are that bureaucracy maximizes organizational efficiency and that, once it is fully established, it is amongst the most powerful and stable forms of social structure. He says, 'Where the bureaucratisation of administration has been completely carried through a form of power relation is established that is practically unshatterable', and again, 'Bureaucracy has been, and is a power instrument of the first order—for the one who controls the bureaucratic apparatus' (Gerth and Mills, 1948, p. 228).

Social workers have been primarily interested in two aspects of bureaucracy; the conflict between bureaucratic and professional types of organization and the influence of bureaucracy upon the personality of its members. In this chapter I shall consider both these topics and then examine three generally held assumptions about the nature of bureaucratic organization.

Professionals and the bureaucracy

From the statement of the bureaucratic model above it is clear that principles of bureaucratic organization are in conflict with the standards of professional practice. There are concrete examples of this. Reiss and Bordua (1967), for instance, comment on the Police Force. On the one hand, Police Officers do have discretion in making decisions which affect the fate of their clients. (The decision to arrest or not is invariably discretionary.) The professional aspects of the Police Force are also important in attracting qualified personnel. Yet, on the other hand, these aspects conflict with the tendency to centralize administration and make decisions at points in the hierarchy above the operating levels of a department. Merton (1957) describes the position of the intellectual in the public bureaucracy:

> The high turnover of expert personnel in public bureaucracies is often the product of the cumulative

frustration experienced by the intellectual who has been previously conditioned to a sense of personal autonomy and cannot abide the visible constraint imposed by a formal organization ... Where he had previously experienced a sense of intellectual autonomy ... he now becomes aware of the *visible controls* over the nature and direction of his enquiries. (pp. 223-4, original italics.)

Bureaucratic and professional forms of organization, however, are not opposed in every respect. They have several elements in common (Blau and Scott 1963). The *sine ira et studio* of bureaucracy is closely paralleled by the emotional detachment of the 'professional relationship'. The professional, like the bureaucrat, is a trained expert only in a strictly (sometimes very strictly) limited field. Security of tenure is an important aspect of the career of both professional and bureaucrat.

The fundamental difference between the two models lies in the difference between the bureaucratic and professional hierarchies of control. The hierarchy of a professional structure consists of a series of advisory relations only. The basic source of discipline is that of self-imposed standards derived from professional training and the norms of the colleague group. An academic in a university, for example, decides upon his own research projects and the content of his lectures. A lawyer decides upon the way in which he will conduct a case. A doctor may seek a 'second opinion' but the final decision on treatment is his own. The professional deals with each case in terms of his own 'professional judgment' and, even if his seniors disagree with his decision, they will defend his right to have made it. The professional refers to few regulations either in dealing with particular cases or in defining his own rights and duties. The professional's contract of employment, for example, is often very vague with unspecified tasks, hours of work, length of holidays, and so on.

The bureaucratic hierarchy, however, is a system of very strict control. The bureaucrat is governed both by the rules and regulations which define his own duties and by those which he applies to each particular case with which he deals. In cases of doubt, he must refer for a ruling to a senior official. He thus has very little discretion and is bound to comply with this ruling. Whereas the professional very much values his autonomy, 'bureaucratic autonomy' is a contradiction in terms.

In social work organizations there are two areas in which professional and bureaucratic forms of organization conflict:

(1) Social work agencies, just like hospitals and universities, have separate structures for (a) administration and (b) professional practice, which correspond to a division of labour within the organization. In universities, academics teach and conduct research while administrators are concerned with student registration, room allocation, budgeting, the building programme and so on. In social work professionals make the casework decision while the administration maintains the files, makes financial arrangements, arranges office accommodation, and the like. But, in spite of this division of labour, there tends to be conflict and confusion at points of contact between the two structures as when a Child Care Officer, for example, arranges payments to foster parents through the boarding out section of his department. While the bureaucrat tends to see the professional as undisciplined, the professional sees 'red tape' as restricting his specialized skills.

One solution attempted by universities as well as social work departments is to make a single appointment to the head of both structures in an attempt to minimize this conflict. A university Vice Chancellor is a senior academic as well as the administrative head. The senior officer of a social work department heads the administration as well as the professional group. The Seebohm Report (1968) makes this proposal for the head of the Social Service Department:

> The objective should be to secure that most of the heads of the social service departments are people professionally qualified in social work ... who have received training in management and administration at appropriate points in their careers, or administrators with qualifications in social work. (para. 620)

Thus, it is clear that the concern professional social workers have shown about appointment of individuals with administrative training to the position of Director of Social Work derives not only from a concern about this one appointment but also about the whole relation between professionals and bureaucratic structures within the organization.

(2) There is also a conflict in social work between bureaucratic and professional standards within the professional groups. As a semi-professional with relatively short periods of training and a comparatively unestablished body of knowledge, a social worker's autonomy is less than we might expect from a study of the more firmly established professions. The social worker is more closely supervised by his seniors than the typical professional. He reports on his activity in greater detail and he is not usually allowed the discretion of refusing his services to a client. They are part of a standard 'case load' referred to him from above.

Thus, the professional ideology of social work is not an accurate description of all aspects of the organizational hierarchy in practice. The role expectations of the social worker, as a professional, conflict with the hierarchical relations within the profession that at times closely resemble those of bureaucratic organization.

Bureaupathology and social work

Members of a bureaucracy tend to take on personality characteristics congruent with this type of organization (Merton 1940). Thompson (1961) refers to these 'Personal behaviour patterns ... which exaggerate the characteristic qualities of bureaucratic organisation' as 'bureaupathology'. This is behaviour which (1) exaggerates dependence upon regulations, (2) exaggerates impersonality in relations, (3) insists on the petty rights and privileges of office, and (4) resists change.

It is a mistake to think that bureaupathology is confined to our typical picture of a bureaucratic administrator or, indeed, to any one particular personality type. As professional groups in a social work agency may operate on the basis of a bureaucratic organization as well as the administrative staff, professional social workers too may manifest bureaupathological behaviour.

Perhaps superiors who insist on their minor rights are most common. For example, one Children's Officer in whose name all letters are sent out of the office, returns drafts even to her senior colleagues for minor stylistic changes. In one instance, Christmas party invitations to foster parents were completely reprinted because the wording had not been checked at a high enough level in the department. Social workers may also stress minor regulations in refusing a client's request. Innovations, too, are often resisted, generally on the basis of 'experience'.

Thompson argues that bureaupathology is a reaction to insecurity by those who are unable to control subordinates within the organization. Certainly in social work there are a number of organizational and wider social reasons for insecurity such as this. There is the strain of conflicting role expectations. Women in our society are often insecure in the superordinate role and a relatively high percentage of social workers are female. Untrained social workers may feel insecure when they encounter subordinates with professional training. The administrator feels threatened by the higher status professional yet the social worker, who is a semi-professional, must also deal with clients who are of a higher social status than himself. A client may point out, for example, that whereas he is a university graduate, the social worker allotted to him is not.

There is, too the usual insecurity of those who are seeking career advancement. The junior social worker is at a particular disadvantage here for, given the current state of social work knowledge, there are few accurate measures of performance which can be used to justify professional promotion. Patients recover, the academic has a publication record, the teacher has qualified pupils. Grading and promotion in a social work organization, however, may well depend upon meeting the 'bureaupathological' requirements of those above. Since it is difficult for the social worker to give evidence of his performance, his conduct within the bureaucracy can be used as a measure of his casework skills. The social worker, for example, who refuses to make minor stylistic changes in his reports is seen as 'unable to accept authority' (Leonard, 1966).

Thus, in viewing bureaupathology as the result of insecurity within the organizational role, we can see that it is not confined to any one particular personality type. This behaviour is likely, either if individuals are placed in superordinate positions yet given only bureaucratic sanctions with which to exercise control, or if they are placed in a subordinate position yet offered only conformity to the bureaucratic rules as a means of gaining promotion. These organizational conditions are present in many areas of social work.

Bureaucracy and size

Bureaucracy is generally associated with large scale organizations. With potential 'Seebohm Departments' in

England and Wales, current mergers of the Health, Welfare and Social Service Departments in some London boroughs and newly integrated Social Work Departments in Scotland, this must be an important consideration in social work thinking.

The size of an organization has been regarded as a controlling factor in the development of bureaucracy. Leonard (1966) shares this view. His comments on bureaucracy begin, 'As organizations increase in size they face characteristic problems', and he continues:

Informal methods of communication and administration become increasingly inappropriate and more formal, rational patterns of interaction are necessary. Thus large scale organisations develop bureaucracy as a means of coping with increased size and complexity. (p. 81)

Claims such as this, however, often lack empirical support. Hall (1963), for example, reports a study in which the concept of bureaucracy is broken down into the six dimensions listed at the start of this section. In studying a range of organizations he found that in only two of these dimensions, (1) a hierarchy of authority and (2) a system of rules for incumbents, did bureaucracy correlate with absolute size. In fact, the link between bureaucracy and size is an assumption based on the over rationalistic approach that we criticized in the orthodox model. The connection between bureaucracy and size is based on the theoretical assumption that a large scale organization can persist as an integrated social structure only if it is bureaucratic.

When we look at studies which examine sufficiently small segments of bureaucracy in sufficient detail we see that the real patterns of activity cannot be explained in terms of the 'formal rational patterns of interaction'. One well-known example of this is the group norms on restricted output in the Bank Wiring Observation Room

(Homans, 1951). Indeed, there is a good deal of truth in the claim that, far from being 'necessary' in large scale organizations, bureaucracies create as many problems as they solve. Every social worker must be aware, for example, of the effect of a formally bureaucratic structure upon the flow of communication. In fact, most organizations which are formally bureaucratic only work at all because they have an 'informal organization'. This is not simply personality deviation from the rules of the blueprint but the real patterns of social behaviour which are independent of the written rules and pictorial charts of the formal organization.

The corollary of statements linking bureaucracy and size is equally misleading. Weber states it thus:

> Only by reversion in every field ... to small-scale organisations would it be possible in any considerable extent to escape its (bureaucracies) influence. (Parsons, 1947, p. 338)

Even if the Seebohm Report is put into effect, of all the authorities in England and Wales, 68% (115) will still employ less than 50 social workers. It would be a mistake to think that, because these organizations are small, at least in comparison with the business corporations and government bodies in which most of the studies of bureaucracy have been conducted, they are free from all aspects of bureaucratic organization. The concept of bureaucracy embodies several dimensions which can be present in varying degrees in the structure of large or small organizations.

Bureaucratization and debureaucratization

Many theories of bureaucracy have been weighted down by a 'metaphysical pathos' (Gouldner, 1961); a foreboding at the supposed inevitable increase in levels of bureaucratization. In asking the question, 'Can a community retain effective control over the bureaucratic organisation?' (Eisenstadt, 1958), most writers have taken a pessimistic view in describing the process of bureaucratization where the bureaucratic organization reaches a state in which it is largely independent of the community in which it was originally established.

This conclusion, if it is justified, has important implications for the bureaucracies of social work. Isolated from the 'grass roots' pressure of their clients, the service ideology is unlikely to be implemented in practice. in the bureaucratized organization the service goals are displaced in favour of the goals of those who control the organization. There are many examples of this. In the employment service studied by Blau (1963) a number of practices were arranged for the convenience of officials and not for the effective job placement of clients. In a comparative study, Sinfield quotes a welfare official as describing the compulsory registration of unemployed clients as 'just another hurdle we make the unemployed jump but it doesn't do them any good' (1968, p. 73). The (then) National Assistance Board refused to publish all their regulations which means that clients were unable to check their assessments (Marsden 1969).

However, Gouldner's comments, from the point of view of the client, are rather more optimistic. He challenges the assumption of an inevitable increase in levels of bureaucratization.

It is the pathos of pessimism, rather than the compulsions of rigorous analysis that leads to the assumption that organisational constraints have stacked the deck against democracy. (p. 80)

As long as the power positions in a social system are not monopolized by one single group, a process of debureaucratization is possible. If groups in close interaction with the organizations are strong enough they will maintain the bureaucracy as a service and limit its autonomy of control. A recent example of this process is the influence of a squatters' association on the policy of a London Borough Housing Department in providing housing accommodation for homeless families. In social work the professional associations are also an important factor in limiting bureaucratic control.

Continuous bureaucratization is thus an over-simplified picture of organizational development. The actual pattern of constant tensions and conflict is more complicated than this. Bureaucratization and debureaucratization may even occur together in different sections of the organization. Different types of client may vary in the degree to which they are able to control the service. The groups I have referred to in this section, the long-term unemployed and fatherless families on National Assistance (now Supplementary Benefits), are in a relatively weak position. The position of foster parents, adoptive parents or the highly educated mentally ill, for example, may be rather different. However, bureaucratization is one possible mode of development for most agencies of social work. A complete analysis of any one situation requires a study of the relative influence of the different groups involved in the organization. Unfortunately, there is as yet very little research on the way in which clients influence the 'service' provided by social work organizations.

Patterns of bureaucracy

A bureaucratic structure does not influence all activity within the organization in the same way. Although bureaucracy has generally been taken as a unitary concept which described activity within all spheres of the organization, Gouldner (1954) in his study of an industrial bureaucracy, suggests that rules within the organization are implemented in three different ways. This can be described in terms of three patterns of bureaucracy within the same organization.

In 'mock bureaucracy' the rules which are imposed on the organization by an outside body are supported neither by supervisors nor by subordinates. In 'representative bureaucracy' both groups support the rules and indeed see themselves as responsible for establishing and maintaining them. In 'punishment centred bureaucracy' the rules are imposed by one group against the wishes of another whose values they may violate.

If we can extend these conclusions from Gouldner's case study, they imply that, regardless of a good deal of 'red tape' throughout the organization, bureaucratic-professional tensions in social work are most likely to occur in those areas patterned on a 'punishment centred' basis. The following are examples from a Children's Department in which I worked for a time.

(1) *Mock bureaucracy*

Regular information from screening interviews with potential foster parents was recorded on a standard form. One fairly complex part of this form had space for recording the dimensions of each room in the applicant's house. This was in accordance with some health regulations which were seen by most social workers as irrelevant to the tasks of the Children's Department. Many officers simply ignored the questions when interviewing the parents. One officer who did carry and use a measure was regarded as a great joke. In spite of the 'red tape' of these rules they produced very little conflict since they were ignored by all groups within the department.

(2) *Representative bureaucracy*

Whenever officers were out of the office, even for a short time, they were supposed to leave a message with the secretary as to where they were. This rule was widely supported and was backed by informal sanctions since it was in everyone's interest to be able to locate other officers in times of emergency, for consultation or for group meetings.

(3) Punishment centred bureaucracy

There were rules governing the financial payments which the Department could make to foster parents, children in care who had left school, and so on. These were criticized by some Child Care Officers who felt that the rules were imposed upon them and that they restricted their professional judgment. They felt that some clients' problems could have been avoided and that their work was made more difficult in a situation in which there is a shortage of foster parents. They were often very critical of these regulations which gave rise to a good deal of tension.

These data (albeit impressionistic) suggest that Gouldner's conclusions can be generalized to social work organizations. They give some clue as to the particular areas of the organization in which professional-bureaucratic conflict is most likely to arise. It is not, as we might expect, simply those areas encompassed by the greatest number of red tape regulations.

Conclusion

This section has summarized the major features of bureaucratic organization. The conflict between this form of structure and the standards of professional practice have been examined as well as the effect bureaucracy has upon the personality characteristics of its members. Finally, some generally held assumptions about the size, development and scope of bureaucracy have been examined in the light of more recent research.

4

Front line organization

It is generally assumed that the power to control an organization rests at the upper levels of the formal hierarchy: with the Medical Officer of Health, with the Children's Officer, the Principal Probation Officer, the Vice Chancellor, the Secretary General, or the Prison Governor.

This was certainly the view advanced by Robert Michels in his famous 'iron law of oligarchy' (1915). He concluded from his study of radical political parties that there is a general tendency in organizations to centralize the executive process. His law asserts that, whether or not there is a formal commitment to democracy, the power to determine operational policy tends to become vested in a small group of leaders at the top of the organization. He called it an 'iron law' because he believed it to derive from the nature of organization as such. As he put it succinctly, 'Who says organisation, says oligarchy' (1962, p. 15).

However, there are contrary examples. In studying mental hospital attendants, Mechanic has titled a paper 'Sources of Power of Lower Participants in Complex Organizations' (1962). Gresham Sykes says of the prison, 'The pressures which tend to shift power from the hands of the guard to the hands of the inmate are often realised in fact' (1961, p. 197). Considerable power may rest with those who occupy positions at lower levels in the hierarchy. Formal authority and effective power do not always coalesce. Michels would agree with this yet we can 'invert' Michels. Whereas he studied formally democratic organizations which were in practice oligarchic, in many social work organizations there is a formal hierarchy of authority but in practice a dispersal of power.

It is this aspect of social work organizations that the concept 'front line organization' helps to describe.

The characteristics of front line organization

In those organizations which refute Michel's iron law there is a general decentralization of the executive process. Power to decide operational policy remains with 'front line units'. These are either individuals or small work groups at the periphery of the structure. Dorothy Smith (1965) refers to this type of structure as 'front line organization'.

Front line organizations have distinct characteristics all of which are important features of field social work agencies, voluntary service organizations, and some types of residential institutions. There are three particular characteristics:

(1) Organizational initiative is located in front line units.
(2) Each unit performs its tasks independently of other units.
(3) There are obstacles to the direct supervision of the activities of such units (Smith, 1965, p. 388).

(1) Locus of organizational initiative

Tasks are initiated for the organization at the front line level rather than by directives travelling down the chain of command. Social workers do not think of casework practice as the application of general departmental rules.

37

The social worker formulates casework objectives in the interview situation with each client.

In some organizations the situation at the point at which the tasks are actually performed may change so rapidly as to render hierarchical initiative impossible. This may be referred to as 'a crisis'—a situation in which events are moving rapidly and the social worker is having to make numerous decisions to initiate courses of action, without consultation. For example, children are received into care in emergency situations, perhaps just as the office is closing on a Friday afternoon. A welfare worker may have to make immediate provision for an elderly person's meals.

In situations such as these front line units work without direct participation by superordinates.

(2) *Locus of organizational initiative*

In front line organizations the individuals, or work group, are functionally autonomous. The labour is not serially divided, as in the production line of a factory, nor is the worker heavily dependent upon the service functions of others. In most casework agencies, once the caseload is established and a client assigned, only one social worker from the agency is directly involved in the case. Even the co-ordinating case conference is redundant where separate social workers deal with each 'problem family'. In a voluntary service organization such as Community Service Volunteers, the projects are largely independent of each other.

This feature of front line organizations is particularly important in the way it affects the structure of communication. In a centrally controlled organization with a detailed division of labour, units towards the centre have an increasingly comprehensive view of organizational activity, whereas units at the periphery have access to information only from within their own sector. In a front line organization peripheral units still have a limited view.

A housemaster in a boarding school, for example, knows little of other houses. But 'pockets of information' develop which also restrict the view of units at the centre. For example, the national offices of voluntary organizations find it difficult to persuade local branches to send in annual accounts. If a Child Care Officer files only brief field visit reports, his Senior finds it difficult to conduct adequate supervision.

McCleary's (1961) study of a prison concludes that information can be equated with power. And March and Simon comment:

Once a pattern of communication channels has become established this pattern will have an important effect on decision making processes. (1958, p. 168)

The typical communication structure of a front line organization is thus an important element in dispersing operational control.

(3) *Obstacles to supervision*

There are major obstacles to direct supervision in front line organizations. Front line staff frequently work in rooms or buildings which are inspected only rarely, and then only at specified times: the teacher in the classroom, the children's nurse in the dormitory, the night nurse in the ward, the prison officer on the landing, the probation officer in the interview room. There is no continuous supervision of day-to-day affairs.

Physical distance also makes continuous supervision difficult. It is hard to supervise social and welfare workers in the field working away from the area office. Most voluntary organizations have a national office but local groups distributed widely. Geographical and temporal dispersal in the loci of action also gives front line operators substantial autonomy. It is even harder to supervise social and welfare workers in the field if they are constantly mobile between cases.

The importance of communications and the rapidly

changing environment of social work practice have already been mentioned. These two factors combine further to restrict supervision. As March and Simon explain, 'Where decisions are made relatively rapidly ... only the information that is locally available is likely to be brought to bear' (1958, p. 169). In front line organizations this information is the front line pocket and over this, central units have very little control.

Control dilemma in front line organizations

In a critical approach to the orthodox model (see Ch. 1) I argued that the official goals of an organization are usually stated in only very general terms and that to understand fully the influence of these 'policy statements' in an organization we have to examine the process by which these are operationalized.

In front line organizations this process is under the control of peripheral units: the field officer, the teacher, the local volunteer. However, this is not to deny that control over general policy in front line organizations is retained by those who occupy positions at the centre: the prison Governor, the Matron, the Headmaster, the executive committee, the Secretary General. They retain, too, public responsibility for standards of performance within their organization as judged in terms of these policy statements. A Children's Officer, for example, is held to be responsible for all the children in the care of his department, even though he may never have met them.

Central units of front line organizations are thus in a dilemma.

> The dilemma of those who occupy control positions is that they are responsible for making policy and maintaining standards of performance for the organisation as a whole, while occupying positions from which this responsibility can least effectively be exercised ... (Smith, 1965, p. 395)

This dilemma is solved by attempts to strengthen the pattern of operational control and reduce the autonomy of front line units. The rest of this section looks at some of the ways in which this attempt is made.

(1) *Control through professional training*

A professional control structure is particularly important in social work organizations. In a process of training controlled by the profession the individual internalizes standards of commitment and acquires levels of competence which ensure that he acts in accordance with a given set of norms even in the absence of intensive supervision. There are strong financial inducements to undertake professional training and senior posts may be open only to those who have been granted this qualification. In another example, teaching, professional training is compulsory in some sectors.

However, it is important to remember that in England and Wales only 40% of social workers are professionally qualified (Seebohm, 1968, Appendix M, Part II). Etzioni also points out that the training of social workers is relatively short (less than five years) and that 'no questions of life and death are involved' (1964, p. 88). Nokes (1967) too, mentions that the welfare professions are unable to give their practitioners the status of the true 'virtuoso' professional. On this basis Etzioni refers to the social work agency as 'semi-professional' and argues that additional controls are likely to be employed.

(2) *Control through communication*

In spite of the front line advantage in controlling pockets of information, central units can attempt control through the structure of communication in several ways (Smith, 1970). First, they can attack these pockets. Such procedures, aimed at securing a 'free flow of upward communication', include requests for regular reports, copies of letters for duplicate files and on-site collection of information. 'Accounting' forms of information may be collected. This is usually attempted in the form of performance statistics. (Although, as Blau (1963) has shown, this can have some unexpected results. This point is described in greater detail in Chapter 10.)

Central units can either widely distribute or limit access to information which comes to the organization from outside sources. It is through the head of a social work department, for example, that information is exchanged with other Local Authority departments, departments of central government, and other organizations.

Finally, because they control the resources for research, production and distribution, central units can 'create' information and control its presentation. Particularly in voluntary organizations with a complex committee procedure, such 'details' as agenda formation, order of presentation and dates of distribution may be crucial.

A number of other control structures may be employed. Supervision may be intensified, as in the visits of Inspectors to schools. Another method is the use of charismatic figures. Front line performance is exposed to the correction and advice of particular leaders. Financial control and the distribution of other resources is also an important sanction. Procedures of recruitment and selection may even be used to exclude some classes of personnel completely from membership of the organization. The constitution, legal regulations and by-laws can also be used to advantage by those who have a fuller understanding of their complexities.

Finally, in organizations in which senior positions are occupied by those who are graduates from within, central units have this general advantage. They can give a much fuller 'account' of the organization as a whole. Those at the periphery often have very little knowledge of the system at the centre.

Conclusion

This section has been concerned with the way in which power to control operational policy is distributed throughout the organization.

Many social work organizations closely resemble the model of a front line organization. There is a formal hierarchy of authority but operational control is located in peripheral units. An organizational dilemma is thus imposed upon those who occupy central positions. As a result of this, control mechanisms develop, designed to restrict the authority of front line units.

In social work organizations, two particularly important controls, amongst others, are professional training and the structure of communication.

5

The total institution

The characteristics of total institutions

There are some groups of organizations that have so much in common that to learn about any one of them we do particularly well to study the others. Such organizations as mental hospitals, boarding schools, prisons, old folk's homes, remand centres and children's homes have been termed 'total institutions' (Goffman 1961).

Not every total institution shares all the common features and some of the features are not peculiar to total institutions. There is, however, a family of attributes, which tends, empirically, to cluster together.

First, attendance for the majority of inmates is compulsory. Physical coercion may be used to enforce attendance. This is most obviously the case in a remand home, prison or borstal, but Townsend (1962) reports that 200-300 people each year are compulsorily admitted to old people's homes. He adds that for each one of these cases there are several more where the threat of compulsion is enough to secure the acquiescence of an aged person. Children at boarding school or in the care of a children's home are seldom in the institution as a result of their own choice.

Second, there are no barriers to divide the normally

separate activities of sleep and other domestic affairs, recreation and work. All these activities are tightly scheduled, all occur within the boundaries of a single limited location and within the order of a single coherent plan supposedly designed to achieve the official goals of the institution. King and Raynes (1968), for example, report on the everyday routine in the lives of severely subnormal children cared for in a hospital ward:

> This regime is changed only slightly at weekends or during school holidays. Get up times, bed times, toilet times, bath times and meal times do not vary much throughout the year. Even at weekends it is only in the afternoon that time is found for the children to play in the yard outside. and then only in the finest weather. (p. 704)

Frank Norman (1969) recalls the routine of a Barnardo's home:

> Get up, wash, make your bed, sweep the floor, breakfast, P.T., morning prayers, classes, lunch, play, classes, play, tea, mow the lawn, evening prayers ... bed, sleep. (p. 48-9)

Thus, third, the organization of the total institution is incompatible with many of the basic patterns of life in society at large. The inmate of a total institution is usually required to conduct his affairs in the company of a large batch of others. In one of the old people's homes studied by Townsend (1962), one room served as dining hall and dormitory for 56 men. Domestic existence within the family is impossible. Inmates of British prisons are not allowed conjugal visits from their wives. Elderly married couples in a home may be unable to share a room. A brother and sister in care may have to live in separate homes. In a total institution the inmate no longer supports himself. Work, in a prison, for example, becomes part of the punishment system. In Pentonville prison, earnings (around 6s. per week) are based on the length of sentence served, and record, as well as on work performed (Morris, 1963). Work is no longer a prime determinant of the inmate's standard of living and style of life. Indeed the whole meaning of work is changed in the total institution.

Fourth, in total institutions there is a basic split between inmates and staff. The echelon principle operates throughout the institutions. Even the most junior member of staff has almost total authority over even the most senior inmate. Mobility between the two groups is impossible and typically social distance is maintained. Staff, for example, may talk in front of inmates as if they were not there. Communication between staff and inmates is stereotyped and inmates may be kept from knowledge of decisions taken about them.

Yet inmates enter the institution in possession of a 'presenting culture', that of their own social networks. And in terms of this culture these features of the organization will appear alien. This culture must thus be eradicated if they are to understand their new role. It is through a process of mortification (the fifth feature) that this is achieved. The inmate must undergo a sudden and sometimes harsh process of initiation. He may lose his usual name and be referred to by surname or number. He may lose his usual appearance. Boarding school housemasters can insist on out-of-date haircuts. The inmate may lose his clothes and personal possessions. In one institution,

Few of the children have possessions or toys of their own, and none has a complete set of clothes which is kept for his personal use. Instead toys quickly become communal property, and clothes are distributed daily, according to approximate size, upon receipt from the laundry. (King and Raynes, 1968, p. 704)

The inmate is controlled by sanctions based on a very

detailed knowledge of aspects of his everyday life. He may even suffer the 'looping effect', the punishment of normal human reactions which follow an original punishment.

A reorganizing system, sixth, is then employed in the total institution to build up for the inmate a picture of his world quite different from that which he would have derived from his presenting culture. Through punishment and reward, the inmate undergoes 'personal reorganization'. Minor privileges are granted and withdrawn. In prison the system of remission and parole rewards obedience to the rules. The positions of 'trustee' and 'prefect' are allotted to those who fully accept the normative standards of higher participants within the institution.

Finally, a distinctive cultural milieu develops within the total institution. There are rituals peculiar to each institution. In one voluntary home, for example,

(The meal) is ended by the matron calling a child to say grace. After this the children stand up, clasp the hand of their neighbour and, turning to them, say 'thank you' (King and Raynes, 1968, p. 706).

A certain amount of distinctive language frequently develops. The argot of prison and remand homes is often noted (Sykes 1958). This again stresses the impermeable aspects of the organization and its isolation within the cultural as well as the social system of its environment.

Social work in total institutions

The concept of 'total institution' is useful in social work, highlighting as it does the way in which the underlying structural characteristics of this type of organization influence social work practice.

First, the total institution typically produces an unusual amount of harsh, even violent behaviour. The description

47

of a 'regimental scrubbing' which used to follow a truancy from Barnardo's is one example:

> A few minutes later two prefects arrived on the scene and escorted me to the bath house ... I was ordered by the two boys to strip naked, they pushed me under a cold shower and scrubbed me with stiff yard brooms (Norman, 1969, p. 117).

Such violence can be explained in terms of the mortification process, an organizational pattern of the total institution, and not simply in terms of the personalities of individual members. When we understand this we cease to 'blame' particular superintendents, governors, nurses, or whatever, and begin to understand the social problems inherent in this type of institution.

Second, total institutions operate in such a way that they produce self-fulfilling prophecies with reference to the way in which clients are defined. The ways in which inmates react to the total institution are likely to be seen by the staff as confirming the diagnosis which originally occasioned the inmates entry into the organization.

For example, inmates react to the process of mortification in one of four ways (Goffman 1961). In 'situational withdrawal' the inmate simply retreats from all the events around him. The 'intransigent' refuses any co-operation with the staff. In 'colonization' the inmate completely accepts his institutional life and seeks never to return to the outside world. In the recently initiated process of prison parole, for example, many eligible prisoners have not applied. A similar reaction is found amongst school-leavers in care who are reluctant to abandon the protection of their children's home. Finally, in conversion, the inmate accepts the staff view of himself and consciously tries to act out the role of perfect inmate.

Now those who withdraw or colonize are likely to appear 'inadequate'. Intransigents will be seen as 'aggressive' or 'unco-operative'. Even those who adopt conversion may appear strange, as, for example, the mental patient who consciously acts out the psychiatric view of himself. In this way the organization itself produces reactions which confirm the original diagnosis. Barton (1966) and others report 'institutional neurosis' amongst geriatric patients, the mentally ill, and retarded adults and children. Such behaviour generally results from conditions prevailing in the institution but is likely to be attributed by staff to the personality characteristics of the inmates themselves. To take another example, in homes for the aged, evidence of 'senility' is in part a function of old age but is also a function of the institution which deprives inmates of their occupation, privacy, identity, and the ability to make even minor decisions about their own future (Townsend 1962).

Third, the impermeable pattern of the total institution is a vital limitation in social work practice. The inmate is not only isolated from his family and friends but from the community as well. A prisoner sees his wife only on the other side of a table during a supervised visit. The days on which children in a home can go out to tea are generally limited. In some institutions the children attend school within the grounds. Residents may remain lonely and socially isolated even if not physically detached. Under 20 of Townsend's sample of old people claimed to have a friend among the other residents. Belknap (1956) reports that visitors to one mental hospital were not allowed to penetrate the environment of the ward but met patients in a special visiting room. Thus the tension between what the organization does and what it must officially say that it does is particularly acute where social work is attempted within total institutions. The social work goals of these organizations are often phrased in terms of restored family relations and a 'normal' return to society at large. Yet because of the impermeable aspect of these organizations this is very difficult to achieve and they often seem to function more as 'storage dumps for inmates' (Goffman 1961).

This last point has been gradually accepted in social work thinking. Increasingly children are boarded out with foster parents. A system of parole for prisoners has just begun. A number of local authorities have grouped flatlets for old people (Min. of Housing and Local Govt. 1968). Some of these have a guest room for relatives who come to stay. These schemes attempt the desegregation of the client or inmate and his wider social relations. The concept of total institution provides a useful comparative framework for describing this change.

Some reservations

In spite of the usefulness of the idea of 'total institution' in guiding social work thinking and focusing research, the concept cannot be applied without some reservations.

(1) The data

The concept of total institution is largely based on secondary material and impressionistic data. In particular Goffman draws on accounts by ex-inmates of their experiences. This gives us only one perspective on life in the institution. In the essay 'On the Characteristics of Total Institutions' (1961) there are thirteen extended quotations from personal accounts by inmates but none from the personal accounts of members of staff, although a great deal of reliable data is quoted from reports of students of these institutions. The research problem is that few accounts by members of staff exist. We should be aware, however, that the nature of the data available may influence the general conclusions.

The way in which Goffman uses personal accounts contrasts, for example, with the use made of prisoners' essays by Morris (1963) in the study of Pentonville Prison. Here the essays are used in appendix to show the perceptions of the prison world which prisoners hold. These perceptions often conflict with detailed findings of the researchers' own study. Inmates' accounts of an organization are best taken not as descriptions of reality but as evidence of the effect of the institution upon the perceptions of inmates.

(2) *Evaluative connotations*

The concept of total institution has acquired heavy evaluative connotations. The equation of children's homes, boarding schools and monasteries with army camps, asylums and concentration camps, means that statements employing the concept tend to be taken as recommendations of social policy rather than statements of sociological description. In spite of efforts to rid the concept of pejorative overtones, total institutions are generally regarded with disapproval. One analysis of the ship is a rare exception (Aubert, 1968).

I have already referred to the dangers in research of adopting one particular view of the goals of the organization, or one particular perception of day-to-day events in the institutional world. Potentially (although not inevitable) similar dangers are involved in employing a value laden concept such as total institution. And this is not only a danger inherent in concepts of disapproval. 'The therapeutic community', for example, is a concept equally laden with the values of approval.

(3) *Significant differences*

In spite of the similarities between different types of total institution, some important differences have still to be spelled out. Total institutions have been defined denotatively, by listing them. This list is justified by establishing common characteristics, but only, as Goffman says, 'with the hope of highlighting significant differences later' (1961 p. 17).

One such difference is the subsequent career of graduates

of the institution. The 'old boys' of some boarding schools may form an important network long after leaving school. A period spent in prison can be an important stage, in making contacts, in the development of a 'deviant career' (Becker 1963). Ex-mental patients, on the other hand, tend to avoid all previous contact with their institution.

Total institutions also differ in the part they play in the life sequence of their inmates. Boarding schools and children's homes are organizations of childhood and socialization. The inmate graduates to a role in the wider society. Geriatric wards, homes for the aged, institutions for the criminally insane, on the other hand, withdraw inmates from society. Often they are never expected to return. We would anticipate this as an important factor in influencing inmates adaptation to the environment of the institution.

A paper by King and Raynes (1968) reports differences in patterns of day-to-day care in otherwise very similar total institutions. In comparing three patterns of care for severely subnormal children 'individualized' patterns occurred in a relatively autonomous institution, less individual attention was given in a ward, part of a large compound hospital, and in a voluntary home, part of a medium-sized compound, a 'mixed' pattern occurred. It seems that autonomy of the organization within a wider social system is a factor that may produce variation in the day-to-day environment of total institutions.

Total institutions differ, too, in the degree to which their barriers are actually impermeable. There are very few institutions indeed which are really completely cut off from the outside world. One prisoner has described, for example, how by obtaining a job as prison cleaner he could see his wife, from a corridor window, in the road below each day. This is just one example of an 'influence from over the wall' (Morris 1963). Newspapers, radio and television, visitors, non-resident staff, new admissions, graduates and tradesmen, all permeate the barriers of the total institution. Boarding school pupils return home for the holidays and long week-ends. Children in care may visit their parents, albeit rarely. Hospital patients do have visitors. Prisoners sometimes escape. The next section of this book, describing the permeable aspects of organizations, will serve as a framework for exploring the effect of this continuous variable on total institutions. For the concept of total institution will only be refined and developed when differences such as these are specified more clearly.

Conclusion

In this section I have outlined the concept of 'total institution'. This concept is useful in social work for the way in which it highlights organizational limitations upon social work practice. Some reservations in using the concept relate to the type of data upon which it is based, the evaluative overtones of the concept, and some significant differences between total institutions which the concept tends to obscure.

6

The permeable organization

The characteristics of permeable organizations

In contrast to the impermeable aspects of the total institution is another group of organizations with very different features. Here the external social networks 'tangential' (Selznick, 1966) to the organization are important in their effects upon the internal structure. It seems helpful to group these organizations in an 'ideal type' referred to as the 'permeable organization'. As well as some statutory agencies of social work this type closely resembles many voluntary social service organizations such as IVS, WVS, Service 9, and CSV for example. It has, too, features in common with the recent developments in residential care that I have already mentioned, such as small group homes for children, grouped flatlets for the aged, and small dispersed hostels for the mentally ill.

The first and most important characteristic of the permeable organization is the fact that membership is voluntary. (Even the definition of membership can, itself, be vague.) Most psychiatric hospitals, for example, now have very few 'certified' patients. Clients come to the organization of their own accord and can leave at will. It is also relatively easy for members of staff to leave and obtain another appointment. Residential accommodation is now less often tied to the job and in Britain at the moment, at least, a shortage of trained social workers makes job mobility easy. For voluntary workers, of course, participation in the activities of the organization is a matter of choice. For example, in one unpublished survey of a British voluntary service organization, 67% of the sample of ordinary members had no contact at all with any regular activity of the organization. A further 10% had contact only rarely. Membership apathy is generally a recurrent theme in the literature on voluntary organizations. Organizational inactivity may even be institutionalized in the category of 'associate member'. A member's level of participation may fluctuate widely and he may even leave and rejoin the organization at will. Thus, at least for clients and voluntary workers and in some respects for professionals too, the permeable organization is an 'enrolment economy'.

A clear division is maintained in the permeable organization between 'work', 'free time activity' and private domestic arrangements. The permeable organization does not encroach upon the family and domestic life of its members. Client contact is restricted to interview and limited visits. Clients and voluntary workers are free to pursue their permanent occupations. I have already mentioned the absence of residential accommodation for staff. The fact that their domestic life is not controlled by the organization is stressed when, for example, field social workers receive extra reward in compensation for weekend duties. In general, membership of a permeable organization places few restrictions upon membership of other social networks in society. Whereas a member of a total institution can never be a member of more than one at a time there is a great deal of multiple membership of permeable organizations. In the survey above, for example, 23% of committee members were members of at least five other voluntary organizations. Old people in local authority grouped flatlets may belong to several social clubs as well as attending church (Ministry of Housing and Local Government 1968).

The boundary maintenance structure of the permeable organization is very weak. In contrast to the high walls, heavy gates and isolation of the total institution the permeable organization is not confined to a single limited location. There may be headquarters or a central office but local groups, area teams and individual members are widely dispersed. In many voluntary organizations many local groups have no premises at all of their own. While we can immediately think of the total institution as the building in which it is housed, the permeable organization cannot be defined in this way. Typically, too, there is ease of access to members of the permeable organization. Staff are thus more likely to be influenced in their conduct by public opinion, sponsors, government bodies and other organizations. The work of the organization often involves co-operation with other agencies. So, whereas internal control may be difficult, the permeable barriers to the organization render supervision by outside bodies relatively easy.

The role structure of the permeable organization is rather more complex than that of the total institution. A role is defined by reference to a number of 'counter positions' (Gross 1958). In the total institution the inmate has access only to those definitions which he is offered from within the institution. In the permeable organization the client can refer to 'significant others' beyond the barriers of the organization. He can appeal to criteria derived from his own culture. For example, in a total institution the inmate is required to use verbal responses (such as 'Sir') and adopt physical postures (such as standing to attention) in relating to members of staff, whoever they are. In the permeable organization clients may distinguish between junior and senior members of staff and relate differently to them. Blau (1963) reports that in one agency clients were more aggressive towards the receptionists than they were towards the interviewers. There are, too, extra-organizational standards for assessing the benefits of the organization. Marsden (1949) quotes one woman as saying:

> The stuff (clothes) they gave us were as black as a fire back. We took it along to the national assistance and we threw it back at them and said 'What the hell do you think that we are?' (p. 203-4)

The 'aggregation process', in which the individual is able to retain his identity and presenting culture, is in sharp contrast to the 'mortification process' of the total institution. In the permeable organization the individual more easily retains his previous definition of himself. He is called by his own name, for example, and he wears his own clothes. In fact the general conduct of the organization is in terms of personal identities rather than official titles. Staff, particularly voluntary workers, are referred to by name and seldom wear uniform. The N.S.P.C.C., for example, had just announced that the uniform of its officers is now regarded as inappropriate to their casework tasks.

In the permeable organization the individual is generally free to schedule his own affairs. As there is no limited location so there is no single scheduled plan. Arrangements are individually made, not for an organizational batch. Social workers visit their clients one at a time and only rarely in consultation with other members of staff. Clients 'drop in' at will. In hostels individuals may come and go as they please. In voluntary organizations even minimal co-ordination invariably recurs as an aim which is not achieved.

Thus, there is no system of personal reorganization. Rather, the presenting culture of clients and staff is incorporated into the cultural system of the organization. Punishment is rare. The sanction of withholding release is without power. There are sanctions of personal intrusion to be derived from a detailed knowledge of every aspect of the client's life. Normative rather than coercive control is used.

The cultural milieu of the permeable organization thus differs only minimally from the culture of the wider social system. The 'release binge phantasy' of the total institution, argot, slang, and 'in' jokes are rare.

These, then, are the major characteristics of the permeable organization. The concept has been constructed as an ideal type 'polar' to the concept of total institution. It is not intended as an accurate description of any one particular organization. It does, however, highlight some internal features of those organizations in which external social networks permeate the barriers of the organization. Together with 'total institution' it also acts as a framework for describing some current changes in social work thinking about institutional care. Some possible effects of a permeable structure in social work organizations are outlined below.

Volunteers in social work

Permeable organizations seem most able to adapt to the use of social service volunteers. There are many social work situations in which professionals and volunteers work together. There are prison visitors, hospital visitors, leagues of hospital friends, 'aunties' to children's homes. At current allowance levels we might even think of foster parents as volunteers. In voluntary organizations salaried professionals are often employed to recruit, train and organize the volunteers, and the Seebohm report (1968) foresees a developing trend in professionals and volunteers working together.

> With the continuing growth of the personal social services it will be more and more necessary for local

authorities to enlist the services of a large number of volunteers to complement the team of professional workers; and the social service department must become a focal point to which those who wish to give voluntary help can offer their services. (para. 498)

The concepts of total institution and permeable organization help us to examine this trend.

In the total institution the volunteer challenges the stability of the organizational barriers. He passes freely through these barriers. He is a part of the institution not subject to staff control. His domestic life is outside the bounds of the institution. He is not a part of the institutional schedule. He retains his cultural identity, of which being a volunteer is itself an important part: a part which is basically alien to the culture of the total institution. He is likely to be seen by inmates as a member of staff and by members of staff as an 'outsider'. Thus, when the volunteer challenges the 'totality' of the institution, staff are likely to react by confining his efforts at voluntary social work to the periphery of the organization.

The prison visitors described by Morris (1963) are one example. Welfare Officers resented the way in which visitors viewed the prisoners. One, for instance, is reported as saying—

... visitors' attitudes to their prisoners don't help because they tend to reassure prisoners that they are not bad fellows at all really. (p. 295)

Uniformed staff were 'scarcely enthusiastic', and the visitors were not allowed access to the prisoners' records. Yet the incorporation of voluntary workers requires not so much changed attitudes on the part of the staff as a change in the 'total' aspects of the organizational structure.

The organizational activity of volunteers is more fitted to the structure of the permeable organization. Here they challenge no existing control relations. They pass freely through the weak barriers. In defining their role their own reference groups are accepted as legitimate 'significant others'. The very free organizational schedule more easily adapts to irregular lengths and levels of voluntary service.

Some consideration has now been given by the Aves Committee (1969), for example, to the position of volunteers in social work. A good deal of discussion has surrounded relations between voluntary and statutory agencies but relatively little consideration has been devoted to relations between voluntary and professional workers within the same organization. It is important to remember in this context that the performance of volunteers depends not only upon their skills and training but also upon the organization.

Precarious values

The legitimating values in the permeable organization are inherently insecure. In any organization agents justify their activity by reference to a series of values. These are more general statements of goals in the organization. I have already mentioned several ways in which the goals of an organization are subject to change but Burton Clark (1956) argues that given certain conditions the values, too, are insecure. The values in social work organizations fulfil all these conditions.

(1) *Values tend to be precarious when they are undefined.* There are numerous textbook statements of the aims and principles of social work. But I have already noted that in the day-to-day life of an agency or institution these values are rarely clearly defined in operational terms.

(2) *Values tend to be precarious when the prestige of agents is not fully established.*
Since social work has the status of a semi-profession, the social worker's claims to authority are less fully estab-

60

lished than those of more highly professionalized groups such as the medical and legal professions.

(3) *Values tend to be precarious when they are unacceptable to the 'host' population.*
In spite of critics' comments (e.g. Sinfield 1969) that social work is rarely radical enough, the values of social work can be new and unacceptable to a community which is required to finance an expanded social service. For instance, the statements that poverty is not merely a function of laziness or that adolescent delinquents need 'help' rather than 'punishment' are, in general, contradictions of the widely held 'common sense' notions.

Impressionistic evidence suggests that precarious values are particularly characteristic of permeable organizations whereas total institutions are relatively immune. An examination of the last two conditions explains why this should be so.

First, whereas prison officers, residential social workers, and mental hospital nurses, for example, have relatively low occupational status in the community at large, in the closed world of the total institution where reference groups are limited their activity can be justified from *within* the organization. Social workers in permeable organizations, however, are constantly made aware of their lower professional status through interaction with a range of more highly professionalized groups such as the legal, medical and psychiatric professions. They may be required to justify the actions *outside* the organization.

Second, where the environment of a total institution may be hostile to the policy of the organization the boundary maintenance structure limits communication so that staff are less likely to be influenced by criticism, and critics are, anyway, less well informed. In the permeable organization, however, agents quickly encounter hostile reaction and this directly affects the conduct of day-to-day affairs.

'Accounts' of the situation

A permeable structure has important effects on the way in which different 'accounts' of the organization are managed.

Clients have their own conceptions of the organization, its agents and its functions as well as their own problems. These are often very different from the definitions of the social workers who must classify clients in a limited number of ways in order to provide appropriate solutions to a set of typical problems. I have already described the way in which staff redefine the inmate world in the total institution. In the permeable organization, however, this process has the following distinctive features:

(1) In the permeable organization clients' and professionals' definitions are heavily influenced by their respective sub-cultures. The individual refers to these throughout his involvement with the organization.

(2) In the total institution redefinition is achieved primarily through coercion, but only normative and remunerative sanctions are available to professionals in the permeable organization. Thus matching together the different accounts of the organization becomes the very delicate and complex process that has been called 'negotiating reality' (Scheff 1968). The social worker must convince the client of the accuracy of the professional's account of the 'real' situation.

(3) In permeable organizations professionals must also justify their account to other agencies and supervisory bodies. Case histories and organizational records are one means by which this justification can be achieved. Thus the reports of social workers are most accurately seen not as 'statements of reality' but as one particular account of the way in which the situation is defined. At the start of the new Local Authority Social Work Departments in Scotland, for example, in one Children's Department, changes were made to case records in order that decisions which had been taken in the past could be justified to

social workers from other settings who might be dealing with these cases in the future.

Just as we cannot understand official statistics unless we understand the way in which they are derived, so we cannot understand records and case histories unless we understand the organizational processes which give rise to these accounts.

Part Two:

Specific organizations

7
Hospitals

At first sight the goal of the hospital appears quite straight-forward: the treatment and eventual cure of patients. However, a full understanding of the hospital requires a closer examination of the goals of the organization as reflected in its operating policies. With this in mind, the conflicts which have been described as implicit in the custodial aspects of psychiatric hospitals are examined. I then look at the multiple goals of training and research as well as treatment, in the general hospital, and the effects of the general hospital's technology and power structures upon the way in which the goals of the organization change over time. Comments on bureaucratic and front line aspects of the hospital then shed some light on the relative position of doctors and nurses. Finally I report on a major survey of one type of hospital that has been described as a total institution.

Goals

It may be argued that many of the studies of psychiatric hospitals are now outdated as descriptions of current prac-tice, particularly if they were conducted prior to the use of tranquillizing drugs. Yet the locked ward and security wing remain features of many hospitals, and in terms of its significance for the organizational structure, the use of tranquillizers may be little more than a functional alternative to physical constraint. Thus, maximum control by the medical and nursing staff, through sedation, regular ward and administrative routines, locked wards, and limited opportunities for individual initiative on the part of patients, are the features of the psychiatric hospital which have developed in the interests of custody and order.

Yet these features are in direct conflict with the therapeutic goals of the institution. Russell Barton (1966), for example, has labelled such 'custodial' features as 'loss of contact with the outside world', 'enforced loss of responsibility', 'bossiness of medical and nursing staff', and 'drugs', as major factors in the incidence of 'institutional neurosis'. In order to change the situation in which the majority of patients are suffering from this 'disease' after only two years in a mental hospital, he makes such suggestions as 're-establish contacts with the family', 'assist in bringing about personalized events', 'distranquillize', and 'produce a friendly, homely, permissive ward atmosphere' (p. 63). For those whose knowledge of the hospital is limited to its formal goals it might come as a surprise that measures such as this require particular innovative social action.

Thus, it has often been argued (e.g. Belknap, 1956) that psychiatric hospitals have 'displaced' their treatment goals in favour of custody and order. This argument, however, assumes, as does the orthodox model, that it is realistic in the first place to suppose that psychiatric hospitals might actually achieve the goals laid down in formal policy statements. Perrow (1965) argues that it is more appropriate to regard the goal of treatment as of symbolic value only with custody and control as the real operative goals of the organization.

As I have already mentioned (Chapter I) the operative goals tell us what the organization is actually trying to do. They are tied to group interests. In a study of voluntary general hospitals in America Perrow (1963) has shown that these operative policies change over time depending upon the controlling power of different interest groups. At first the hospitals were dominated by trustees who administered the finances upon which the hospitals depended. At this stage the hospitals were primarily used as instruments of social philanthropy. In the second stage, as a result of increasing technical complexity, medical staff dominated hospital policy. Here emphasis was placed on high technical quality, particularly in teaching and research. The goals of teaching and research in a hospital may well conflict with those of individual patient care if major resources are devoted to areas of research simply because they are prestigious in the eyes of the scientific community. This has been the basis of much recent comment on developments in heart transplant surgery.

In the third stage, as a result of increasing administrative complexity, professional administrators came to dominate hospital policy. In this stage operative policy stressed financial solvency, administrative efficiency and a cautious approach to such new forms of care as intensive therapy units or home care programmes. This is in line with the general findings on the conservative influence of bureaucratic administration upon organizational innovation and reform.

But the operative goals of a general hospital are not merely a function of the power position of groups within the hospital. They too are, in part, a function of the social environment upon which the hospital must depend for support. The general hospital depends upon its environment for a charter to operate, for instance, trained personnel, operating funds, capital grants, a supply of patients and the co-operation of other statutory and voluntary organizations. In the goal setting process of the general hospital, then, groups in the local community may be important. The local medical community may play a part since the support of medical practitioners in the area is important for the hospital (Thompson and McEwen, 1958). A 'favourable public image' is also important. While the hospital's prestige may rest upon the quality of its services, it is not always possible for the public readily to evaluate this service. In this case the hospital may develop value laden symbols which bear no necessary relation to the quality of patient care. Examples here, are the number of medical students undergoing training, details of research projects conducted at the hospital, the 'frills' of medical care such as telephones, television sets, long visiting hours and services to private patients (Perrow, 1961a). In this way the 'salient publics' of a general hospital exercise some external control over the organization's operative goals, although the form and degree of contact between a hospital and its public varies widely, of course, between different hospitals.

With changes, then, in the social environment of the hospital and with changes in the hospital's technology, the power base for controlling operative goals moves from the trustees to the medical professionals, to hospital administrators; all this while the formal goals of the hospital remain unchanged. Although trustees are not an important part of the British hospital system, the relation between professionals and administrators has widespread implications. We can look at this relation in more detail if we examine the general hospital as a bureaucratic organization.

Bureaucracy

The doctor, together with the lawyer, has often been quoted as the classic example of the independent professional. Now, the doctor in the hospital may well become the model for organizational professionalization. We can understand his organizational position if we contrast the Weberian model of bureaucracy with the work requirements, norms and values of physicians as a professional group.

The general hospital has much in common with organizations based upon a bureaucratic pattern. There is a finely graded authority hierarchy, symbolically expressed in the styles of dress. Cohen (1964), for example, notes the 'senior hospital staff in full regalia' (page 7) and comments:

> In the nursing world uniform denotes rank with subtler nuance than in the army. Sergeants only bear an extra stripe. Sisters rejoice in frillier caps, bunchier skirts, more buttons and longer sleeves. (page 45)

Detailed written rules govern the lives of patients, nurses, doctors and administrators. Visiting hours, ward routines, admission procedures, treatment procedures—such topics as these are the subject of hospital regulations. The division of labour is laid down in established areas of competence. A hospital may even be characterized by the impersonality of a bureaucratic system. Cohen begins her book, admittedly devoted to answering the question 'What's wrong with the hospitals?', by describing the highly routinized admissions procedures of one hospital, procedures that could be quite inappropriate for the individual case. But, as she says, 'rules were rules' (page 7).

All this is in sharp contrast to the patterns of autonomy and individualized practice that are the norms of the medical profession. The hospital, then, actually involves built-in conflicts between the incompatible bureaucratic and professional systems. Yet in the hospital, organizational mechanisms have emerged that serve to reconcile these potentially discordant elements. There is a dual authority structure (Smith, 1958). The hierarchy of positions entails two different types of control relationship which vary according to whether the area of work is professional or administrative in nature. Only in the realm of administration is the hierarchy referred to authority relations. In the realm of professional work the hierarchy refers only to advisory relations (Goss, 1963). Thus, in the organization of authority amongst hospital doctors the bureaucratic standards are reconciled with professional values through dual control systems within a single hierarchy of positions.

Yet while the doctors are in a very powerful strategic position, partly through the high prestige of their professional status, nurses as a semi-professional group are in a very much weaker position within the organization. They are closely controlled both by the hospital bureaucracy and by hierarchical relations within the nursing profession. Also, as Katz (1969) notes,

> There is considerable antagonism between physicians who want dependable servile nurses and nurses who want professional dignity and autonomy. Physicians obviously have the upper hand. (page 74)

The nurses' major source of autonomy in control lies in their position as front line units. This, as we shall see in the next section, is rather more significant in the psychiatric ward than it is in the general hospital.

Front line organization

In the psychiatric and general hospital the ward is the primary locus of organizational initiative. It is in ward units that patients are grouped on the basis of the type of problem they present and their probable response to treatment. It is, too, through the ward units that treatment is offered and the daily routines of the patient's life are managed. In forming their treatment tasks ward units remain largely independent of each other and there are major obstacles to supervision. In comparison with the wards of a psychiatric hospital, however, especially the locked wards, the ward of a general hospital is a relatively public place. Even here, however, visiting in most general hospitals is limited to specific times, patients are not allowed to wander from one ward to another, and nurses and doctors would expect to be found only on those wards to which they were assigned.

So within the ward as a front line unit (Smith, 1965) nurses have control over the hospital's operative policy, both in the tasks of patient care and, in the locked wards, in the task of custody and control. In particular they control the flow of communication, with the ward as a 'pocket of information'. Communications tend to be channelled within the occupational groups of those who work together on the ward (Wessen, 1958). The wards tend to become self-contained units, there being little communication with other units. Consequently the nurses' ability to control this flow of information is an important source of power for a group that is otherwise of comparatively low status in the hospital hierarchy. As Stanton and Schwartz conclude (1954),

Power includes the ability to command relevant reports, otherwise it is meaningless. The person high in the hospital hierarchy can know only little at first hand and is totally dependent upon those about him—usually those below him in the hierarchy—for his ability to make decisions ... it is apparent, then, that the question of selection is a critical one. (p. 289-290)

Total institution

In this section on the hospital organization we have so far been concerned with psychiatric and general medical hospitals. Both as a topic of welfare planning and sociological research, however, there is a third type of hospital that has, up to now, been comparatively neglected : the hospital for the mentally subnormal. This is an institution which is of particular interest to the sociologist of organizations for in its encompassing character and with its barriers to social intercourse with the outside world it approximates most closely to the ideal type total institu-

73

tion. As Morris (1969) concludes from her extensive survey of this type of organization:

> We believe that our empirical data illustrates very clearly the degree and extent to which subnormality hospitals are isolated not only geographically and socially, but also from the mainstream of both medical and educational advances. (p. 292)

This isolation is a function of the total features of this type of institution.

First, although the 'role stripping' may be attentuated in this type of hospital since the majority of patients have, in any case, been precluded from playing significant autonomous roles prior to their entry, the admission procedures do function to redefine the patient's 'significant others' and image of his own 'self'. Many hospitals, for example, discourage relatives from visiting for the first few weeks following admission. Although justified on the grounds that it might upset the patient it serves to emphasize the distinction between family and institutional life. In 44% of the hospitals studied by Morris the clothes of patients newly admitted were returned home. There is, then, an overall redefinition of the patient's status. 'Irrespective of his chronological age he is defined as a child and the hospital is defined as being *in loco parentis*' (p. 188).

As in other total institutions 'work' and 'leisure' lose their usual meanings. 48% of the adult patients either had no occupation or worked only on the ward, and of the patients' time on the wards Morris comments, 'the great majority spent their time sitting, interspersed with eating' (p. 173).

The operative custodial goals of the institution also contribute to the overall total characteristics. Sanctions play an important part in maintaining a quiet and orderly regime. Stopping parole, stopping entertainments and reducing pocket money are the three punishments most commonly used, but there is, too, widespread use of drugs as an alternative to sanctions. Their use is often custodial rather than therapeutic (p. 174).

Perhaps the clearest indicator of the impermeable barriers of hospitals for the subnormal is the fact that of all patients in Morris's sample 37% had never been visited nor gone home, in the year preceding the research.

Subnormality hospitals are, then, by and large, total institutions. Any attempt by the world outside to impinge upon the world of the institution is a threat to the social equilibrium of the regime in which order is seen by the staff as such a vital component. The data presented by Morris is the sort of data that continues to justify Goffman's claim that total institutions exist in a society as 'dumping grounds for inmates'.

8
Schools

'The aims of education' is an endless topic of conversation within the teaching profession and there can be few organizations in which the goals are as vaguely stated and hotly disputed as those of the school. This complexity has an important effect upon definitions of appropriate compliance relations between pupils and teachers. The operational goals of the school emerge from the way in which this organization resolves two basic dilemmas. First, how can administrative control be reconciled with the professional autonomy of the teacher, and, second, how can families and schools work closely together without challenging the school's organizational structure (Litwak and Meyer, 1968)? These are the topics with which this section will be concerned.

Goals

Formal goals of the school are invariably diffuse. They are stated in general terms such as 'moral training', 'social training', 'preparation for occupation', or 'occupational training'. Musgrave (1968) points out that they tend to reflect those 'goal areas' that have historically been of continual importance in the growth of the British educational system as a whole. The Church, very powerful in the field of education, (examine, for example, the Education Act of 1944), has encouraged the pursuit of religious goals. Political forces have undermined the early nineteenth century concept of élitist education in favour of egalitarian goals. Industrialists, on the other hand, have increasingly argued in terms of economic goals for a formally educated labour force and for developments in scientific and technical education. Yet in spite of these pressures each headmaster within the English and, to a lesser extent, the Scottish educational systems, has a high degree of independence to develop these principles within his own school.

It is at this organizational level that many of the conflicts implicit in abstract statements become apparent. In drawing up the timetable, designing the curriculum, distributing limited resources such as laboratory space, project equipment, new books or private study time, in allocating trained staff to particular classes— in all these areas the demands of egalitarianism and 'a general education' are often in direct conflict with the winning of those formal qualifications that will later fit pupils into the occupational structure.

The importance of the schools' goals may also be differentially perceived. Many teachers tend to see their jobs in terms of subject instruction (Musgrove and Taylor, 1965) and moral training. Sugarman (1967) describes how the conduct of working-class children is affected if they do not share these values. Alternatively 'progressive' heads may meet with much opposition from parents who seek 'paper qualifications' for their children.

Apart from conflicts between these goals there may also be conflicts in putting into practice just one of these objectives stated at a general level. For example 'moral education' may be cited by one group of teachers at a girls' school to oppose any joint activity with a nearby school for boys, while another group of teachers may take the very same principle to imply an advanced programme of sex education. Finally peer group sub-cultures may have an important effect upon the formal goals of the school organization. While the school is clearly a major institution for socializing children into the standards of the adult world, it is also an important agent of peer group socialization (Coleman, 1961). The norms and values of the pupil sub-culture are often at variance with those of the staff world, a fact which is particularly significant when the student sub-culture either redefines formal punishments as marks of distinction or else wields controls that are more powerful than those of the formal system.

The way in which these conflicts are resolved or persist within the school organization depends upon the power positions of administrators and head teachers, teachers, pupils and parents. We can begin to examine these factors by looking at the compliance relations and the bureaucratic and total aspects of the school's organization.

Compliance

Since the pupils' immediate goals often conflict with those procedures through which teachers are attempting to implement the educational goals of the school as they define them, the compliance relation (the relation between power and involvement) between pupil and teacher is an essential feature of the whole control system of the school organization. Etzioni (1961) describes schools as having moved from a basis of coercive to normative compliance relations in recent years. The merits of the two systems are often debated in prescriptive terms (e.g. Shipman, 1968). Much of the discussion, however, has not been very helpful because it has generally assumed that the social structure of the school involves only congruent types of compliance relations. Some of the problems and complications of teacher-pupil relations can most helpfully be examined in the light of incongruent types.

First, relations are complicated in schools by the varying definitions of appropriate forms of power held by different teachers. Some teachers rely on coercive measures more than others. Some rely on normative measures more than others. Thus the consistent involvement of pupils, whether alienative or moral, will produce the respective incongruent types of compliance relation (7 and 3 in Table 2) if they are switched rapidly from one regime to another.

Second, while teachers primarily rely on coercive or normative power, calculative involvement may be very important for some children, particularly those who are studying for public examinations. (Thus the incongruent types of compliance relation 2 and 8, Table 2.) And it is not only examination qualifications that pupils have to gain. While a 'good' report or job reference may be seen by the teachers as an accurate evaluation, the pupil may well regard it as a 'reward' for conforming behaviour. Similarly, pupils may develop their extra-curricula school activities in order to present an impressive list on a subsequent curriculum vitae. The calculative basis of this involvement may be overlooked by teachers if the meaning that they attach to this behaviour is not the same as that of the pupil.

Bureaucracy

The deficiencies of compliance theory in coping only with the dichotomous relations of a two class model (see Chapter 2) are evident when we attempt to examine the whole system of hierarchical relations in the school involving local authorities, head teachers and inspectors as well as teachers and pupils. In this particular respect schools may be viewed as bureaucratic organizations.

It is true that bureaucratic elements are found in the school system in only 'rudimentary form' (Bidwell, 1965). Although a career structure exists, many teachers, especially women, spend only a few years in the profession. Indeed, in recent salary negotiations the distinction has been made between those who are career teachers and those who are not. Neither is the impersonality of bureaucratic practice generally a feature of teaching. But some features of the bureaucracy remain. There is a clear hierarchy of promotion for teachers in schools, and as schools increase in size the number of grades in the hierarchy tends to increase also. There is too a division of labour with the work divided among specialists involving heads of department and posts of special responsibility within the subject groupings. Through this centralized system the head teachers may delegate particular functions. 'Administration' emerges as a separate task, often the charge of the Deputy Head who arranges such things as the school timetable or the holding of public examinations. Musgrave (1968) notes, too, the amount of behaviour in educational positions that is standardized according to formal rules, in particular rules surrounding the conditions of employment.

The teacher is subject to this hierarchical authority system. Often he is not free to arrange his own syllabus, timetable or hours of work. Head teachers and Her Majesty's Inspectors at least make an attempt to supervise the teaching practice and assess the teacher's work. The theoretical basis of a teacher's work is also subject to change as a result of research in which he himself plays no part. Head teachers and local authorities make decisions on promotion and even school governors may exercise some degree of control through the procedures of staff recruitment. External examiners exercise some control through their ability to pass or fail a teacher's pupils.

At higher levels in the system there are similar restraints. Headmasters must accept the overall educational policy laid down by the local authority: the details and timing, for example, of 'going comprehensive'. Within the inspectorate itself hierarchical patterns persist.

In the process of bureaucratization problems previously treated on an individual basis tend to become routinized because they must be dealt with by one of a limited number of standard procedures. One American study (Cicourel and Kitsuse, 1963), for example, which examined the impact of organizational procedures on the careers of school students found that the bureaucratization of the system severely limited individual variations in patterns of self-development and social and occupational careers. In the interests of 'administrative efficiency' standard forms of reporting and neat sets of examination grades are often encouraged. But if parents, teachers and pupils then adopt patterns of behaviour to conform with these 'labels', indices of performance which are bureaucratic in origin can become determinants rather than reflections of the pupil's performance.

There is a similar danger in the use of a limited number of standard categories for classifying 'cases' in social work practice.

Front line organization

In spite of the patterns of hierarchical control it would be an oversimplification to describe the organizational structure of schools simply as bureaucratic. A distinctive feature of schools is the combination of bureaucratic tendencies with a particular 'structural looseness' (Bidwell, 1965).

Teachers share those problems common to all professional persons in bureaucratic organizations. Conflicts arise, for example, when a head teacher ignores the professional independence of his staff. The head as well as the teacher commands, it is true, sanctions that may be used to establish his own definition of the situation, yet invariably the teacher is successful in securing a good deal of unrestricted autonomy in his professional practice. Certain structural features support the teacher's isolation and functional independence.

In many areas the teacher operates as an autonomous front line unit within the organization. The locus of organizational initiative remains largely with the teachers and, given the confines of the individual classroom, there are major obstacles to the direct supervision of the teacher's activities. There are, too, many areas in which a teacher can perform his tasks quite independently of other teachers in the school. The rhythm of decision-making in schools is intermittent and infrequent in comparison with many other types of organization (Lortie, 1969). Not only do teachers meet their students in separate rooms, these rooms may be widely dispersed throughout separate buildings, particularly in comprehensive school systems which have not been purpose built. All these factors, together with the perpetual reappraisal of appropriate teaching techniques, limits the control potential of a teacher's superiors.

Lortie concludes, 'perhaps the schools of the future will be marked by chronic tension between organisational and professional controls' (page 46). Certainly the school as an organization continues to exist on the delicate balance between the hierarchies of its bureaucratic aspects and the professional autonomy of its teachers.

Total institution and permeable organization

The second major dilemma that has to be faced by the school is the relation between the pupils' families and the school organization. This has also been described in terms of a 'balance theory' (Litwak and Meyer, 1966). On the one hand, families and schools must work closely together, yet on the other hand excessive intrusion on the part of the family into the life of the school presents a serious challenge to the authority structure of the school organization.

First, we can look at the ways in which families and schools are brought closer together. These procedures permeate the barriers of the school organization. Litwak and Meyer have presented an empirical typology of these 'mechanisms of co-ordination' between the school itself and the family, the school's most important external primary group.

The school may attempt to develop links with its social environment through local community leaders. In England the recruitment of some school governors is a very limited attempt at this approach. In the Settlement House approach the facilities of the school may be used by the pupils' families. This is attempted when the school buildings are part of the local community centre. Voluntary organizations such as the Parent Teacher Association may also be used as an important link between family and the school and occasionally schools employ a form of the mass media to circularize all parents with particular information. In the Detached Worker approach the caseloads of a number of social workers attached to the school consist entirely of pupils and their families. School welfare officials also have the authority to visit homes and demand compliance with statutory attendance regulations. Finally, the pupils themselves, as members of both, act as the most obvious link between school and family.

Through these mechanisms then, the boundaries of the school organization are permeated in an attempt to maintain parent interest. From the point of view of the teacher, however, they may also represent a very serious threat. One teacher, for example, has been quoted by Becker (1961) as saying,

I don't think a parent should try and tell you what to do in your classroom. I don't think that's right and I will never permit it ... so I would never let a parent interfere with my teaching. (p. 244)

From 60 detailed interviews with teachers in America, Becker draws the conclusion, the school is for the teacher, then, a place in which the entrance of the parent on the scene is always potentially dangerous ... the parent appears as an unpredictable and uncontrollable element, as a force which endangers and may even destroy the existing authority system over which (the teacher) has some control. (pp. 245, 251)

The teacher has available a number of devices for dealing with the 'parent problem'. First, he can appeal to the headmaster, who is expected to 'back the teacher up'. Second, he can appeal for support to his colleagues. Certainly it is not normal in schools for teachers to criticize each other in front of either pupils or their parents.

The most secure protection is offered, however, to those teachers who work within the environment of a total institution. The more a school resembles the ideal type of a total institution the greater is the degree of control that the teacher is able to exercise. Cut off from its social environment, a boarding school in term time limits its contact with parents to a small number of highly formalized occasions such as speech day, sports events and perhaps visiting at weekends. In this respect, at least, the problems faced by teachers in total institutions are very different from the problems faced by those who teach in, say, a progressive urban primary school.

Thus, to counteract outside influences structures have developed in schools whereby much of their everyday work is either protected or hidden from public view. The particular organizational procedures involved vary between types of school, but underlying them all the relation between the family group and the teacher's authority is the same very delicate balance.

9
Prisons

Total institution

However impermeable may be the social boundaries of the psychiatric hospital, the boarding school, or the residential social work institution, there are few organizations in which the total features of the institution are as blatantly expressed as in the high walls of the prison.

The prison, then, very closely resembles the pure type total institution. Its boundaries encompass all sleeping, playing and waking hours of the involuntary inmates. The individual prisoner is but one of this batch. He is often assigned a number rather than a name and even on admission, 'the convicted man coming into prison normally arrives with a group of others' (Morris, 1963, p. 102). His everyday life is a matter of routine. As Morris describes the day in Pentonville:

> For the ordinary prisoner, the early part of the day is essentially similar—washing, shaving, slopping out and breakfasting. By 9.30 he is out in the exercise yard, and by 10.00 a.m. in his workshop. Labour normally lasts ...

and so on, until,

> ... at 9.30 the lights are put out for the night. (p. 105)

Only such normally minor events as taking a bath, going to a film, or attending church disturb the inevitable monotonous regularity of the institutional regime. And even these events may be regulated in detail by the minute provisions of the prison rules. As an example, Johnston (*et al.*) (1962) devote a section of their reader to a lengthy quotation from the rule book of one American prison. Rule 1 is, 'your first duty is to strict obedience of all rules and regulations'. Other examples are Rule 6, '... making faces or insulting gestures will not be tolerated ...' or Rule 50, 'On entering the chapel, you will march erect with arms at your sides.' The list of offences includes not only such 'serious' activities as 'creating a disturbance', or 'refusing to obey', but also such details of everyday life as 'bed not properly made', 'hair not combed', 'throwing away food' and 'staring at visitors' (pp. 87-91).

As in other total institutions the procedures at admission symbolically serve to deprive the new prisoner of his own presenting culture. He takes off his own clothes, and deposits with the admissions' officer all his own belongings. Clad in a prison dressing gown he must then take a bath in the adjoining bathhouse (Morris, 1963, p. 103). 'Personal reorganization' is attempted through the use of punishments (such as solitary confinement and bread and water diet) as well as rewards (particular privileges and, above all, remission of sentence). In describing, however, the compliance relations within the prison I shall be examining the effectiveness in practice of this formal system of control.

The final feature of the total institution, a distinctive cultural milieu, is also particularly pronounced within the prison organization. In this society of captives the parlance of the inmates, prison argot, is 'pungent, vivid, racy and irreverent' (Sykes, 1958, p. 84). There are 'rats' and 'squealers' (informers), 'barons' and 'merchants' (traders, often in tobacco), and 'wolves', 'punks', and 'fags' (homosexual roles). Even with restrictions on inter-prisoner communications, signs, gestures and complex systems for carrying messages via 'kites' (messengers) give rise to a culture of communication that can, on occasions, be scarcely intelligible to those not acquainted with this inmate sub-culture of the prison organization.

This sub-culture has often been described as a reaction to the deprivation of the total institution. Certainly the 'pains of imprisonment' (Sykes, 1958) involve rather more than the simple deprivation of liberty and can have important and unanticipated effects upon the way in which the prisoner defines himself and copes with the strains of his situation.

First, in modern western culture, in which material possessions are such an important part of an individual's self-image, the deprivation of goods and services means more to the prisoner than simply material discomfort. He sees himself defined not only as an offender, but also as a failure. Deprived, too, of heterosexual relations the prisoner's conception of himself as a male (or herself as a female) is brought into question. Morris found Clemmer's 1940 account of sexual patterns in a prison community still a fairly accurate representation of Pentonville in 1963. In *Society of Women* Rose Giallombardo (1966) gives a detailed account of the adoption of the male role in homosexual 'marriages' among the inmates of a women's prison. Finally, in depriving the prisoner of autonomy, his status as an adult is challenged. The inmate then, must find a means to cope with the situation in which he is thrust back into childhood helplessness, for the experience to which prisoners are subjected extends well beyond the limited fact of restricted freedom of movement.

One reaction which has been described as an attempt to cope with this situation is that of 'prisonization' (Clemmer, 1958). In many forms of institutional behaviour the individual withdraws into his own isolated world. The prisoner, however, having rejected the codes and values of the formal organization, tends to seek status by adopting

87

the norms and values of a strong inmate sub-culture. This deviant sub-culture, then, functions within the organization to cope with the pains of imprisonment and the role definitions imposed upon inmates by their total institution. As we shall see in a later section this culture seriously undermines the effectiveness of the prison's formal goals.

Compliance

A vast power differential is often thought to characterize the prison's social system. Unlimited means to control the inmate population seem to lie in the hands of prison officials. The prison officer seems to have total monopoly over the legitimate means of coercion. Indeed, at first sight, the prison appears the classic example of an organization based upon coercive compliance relations. Yet on closer examination the total power of the prison officer is in practice an illusion and much of the control that he does exercise is utilitarian rather than coercive. In practice the official mechanisms of social control are limited (Sykes, 1958, Cloward, 1960).

Unable to depend upon moral commitment to any official normative standards, the formal prison system relies upon coercive controls of physical restraint, solitary confinement, and (in the extreme case) corporal punishment, and to a lesser extent upon the remunerative rewards of privileges and remission. While physical force may be useful in an individual case, as a regular means of maintaining order it is basically inefficient. It is generally impractical in terms of the staff–prisoner ratio. (In Pentonville, for example, there are 224 staff to 1,265 prisoners Morris, 1963.) It encourages violent retaliation and it is inappropriate for the effective performance of any complex task. The effectiveness of the remunerative system is also undermined by the way in which it is administered in most prison systems. The distinction between a privilege and a right is often confused. Privileges, particularly remission, are granted as a right and subsequently withdrawn, as the results of an offence. Administered in this way privileges are seen by prisoners not as rewards to be won, but simply as another source of potential deprivation; alternatives, that is, to the existing coercive sanctions. As Sykes describes this process the prisoner finds himself unable to win any significant gains by means of compliance, for there are no gains left to be won. Consequently the prison officer is unable to depend upon the prisoner's normative sense of duty, in many areas he is aware that brute force is inadequate, and he often lacks an effective system of legitimate rewards. A good deal of research has indicated that order is in practice maintained in the prison through a more informal remunerative system.

The prison officer in close contact with the prison population day after day can remain aloof and impersonal only with difficulty. He thinks not only of today, but also of tomorrow when he will be heavily dependent upon the prisoners for the satisfactory performance of his own duties. The officer, himself a relatively lowly member in a hierarchy of authority, will be evaluated in his own performance in terms of the conduct of the men he controls. Particularly in matters of routine the officer relies upon the prisoner for his regular co-operation. Morris (1963) gives an example from the Pentonville Reception Hall:

> In theory, he (the prisoner) may be locked inside one of these lavatory-like structures, but the effort involved in locking in 20 or 30 men at a time, only to unlock them in a short time later, is normally by-passed. (p. 103)

There is a reciprocal relationship. In return officers, for example, may overlook particular offences. Morris reports that in Pentonville it is likely that some of the pornographic literature was imported by members of the prison staff. Again officers ignore 'flashes' between Pentonville

89

husbands and their visiting wives. As Sykes has put it, officers may buy compliance at the cost of tolerating deviance.

In conclusion, we do not intend to imply that the formal authority structure of the prison is totally ineffective. Much of the research does suggest, however, that in the day-to-day life of a security prison, remunerative power and calculative involvement are quite as important as the formal descriptions of coercive and normative types of compliance relation. The conflicts which are in any case implicit in these descriptions can be studied in greater detail if we examine the goals of the prison.

Goals

'The purpose of the training and treatment of convicted prisoners shall be to encourage and assist them to lead a good and useful life' (Home Office Prison Rules, 1964, Rule 1). However we might come to define assistance for a good and useful life, it is unlikely that the operative goals of the prison could really be described in this way. One of the main reasons for this is that the complex operational goals of the prison emerge in practice from a direct conflict between coercive and treatment models of the organization implicit in the dual formal goals of custody and reform. Just as there is a dual authority structure in the hospital so we may think of the prison as two principal hierarchies devoted, on the one hand, to the custodial role of keeping the prisoner secure, and, on the other, to the treatment role of serving the inmate as a client (Cressey, 1965). The two structures have entirely different and largely contradictory purposes.

In the treatment model the prisoner, as a client, is expected to consent to the treatment programme. Compliance relations are normative. In a custodial model coercion is implied and this is the basis of compliance. Yet in practice, as I have described, remunerative factors are really important. In their patterns of communication and decision-making, the two models also conflict. In the custodial model communications are restricted as far as possible to formal rules and commands. Any area in which prisoners have autonomy to make their own decisions represents a threat to security and order. In the treatment model, however, maximizing autonomy is vital in the treatment process. A free flow of communication is also an important part of the decentralized decision-making structure. Finally the whole conception of 'misconduct' is basically very different in the custodial and treatment models. In the former, it is seen as deliberate, to be punished and more closely supervised in the future. In the latter, however, almost all misconduct including the criminal act itself, is seen as unintentional, perhaps even unconscious, the function of personality factors which can be cured in a treatment programme.

The recent history of penology in Britain is sometimes described as a gradual move from the custodial to the treatment model. However, changes which have followed the Mountbatten Report (Hodgson, 1969) have made it clear that this process is not a single one way historical trend. At any point in time the operative goals of the organization are a function of the delicate balance between conflicting pressures to implement the formal prison goals of custody and reform.

A second major factor in examining the divergence between official and operative goals in the prison is the impact which the inmate social system has upon the prisoner. We have mentioned this in describing the process of prisonization, but as Clarence Schrag (1954) comments:

Ineffectiveness of our penal institutions as therapeutic agencies is generally explained in terms of inadequate treatment facilities, inferior qualifications of administrators, of the crimogenic characteristics of inmates. The social climate of the prison and the inter-personal relations among the inmates have received less attention. (p. 37)

This study concludes tentatively that leadership in the informal prison hierarchy is exercised by the criminally mature inmates who are serving long sentences for crimes of violence. Hostile informal organizations are particularly likely if there is a stress upon the custody goal of the prison (Berk, 1966). Socialization for many prisoners may be no more than the process of acquiring the skills and attitudes for further, perhaps habitual, criminal behaviour. As a woman recently released from prison after a twelve month sentence for fraud has been reported as saying, 'All I learned in Holloway is how to steal a car, how to forge a Post Office Book, and how to perform an abortion' (Hodgson, 1969).

However, while this is the sort of data that has given rise to the popular theory that prisons are best described as 'schools of crime' and while this theory has received a good deal of support in the research literature, it would be a mistake to imply that prisons are invariably characterized by inmate solidarity. In one Norwegian correctional institution, for example, though deviant norms certainly existed, they were to an important degree uninstitutionalized (Mathiesson, 1965). The more common reaction was that of individual 'censoriousness'. Here the inmate defined the member of staff as the 'real' deviant. This, it is argued, is an alternative way of coping with the pains of imprisonment. Yet here too, the institution fails to impose upon the inmate its own definition of the situation as set out in formal policy statements.

Conclusion

In this section I have examined the inmate sub-culture as an unanticipated consequence of the prison as a total institution. I have also examined the defects of total coercive power. Together with the implicit conflicts between the formal goals of custody and reform, these features produce a structure in which, in the formation of operative goals, the inmate social system is as significant an influence as the formal prison structure.

10
Social work organizations

Bureaucracy

I have already discussed, both in a number of specific contexts and generally, the differences between bureaucratic and professional forms of organization and the way in which professional persons who work within bureaucratic organizations are subject to socially structured tensions. In social work organizations these tensions are particularly acute and while in some areas they may persist and act as a constant source of conflict, there are some organizational mechanisms which do have the social function of coping with these tensions and lessening conflict. Thus, in this section, I will first examine some features of the social work profession which tend to intensify these tensions. Blau's account of the use of statistical records of performance will then provide an example of the way in which bureaucratic control of social workers can affect their service to clients. Finally, some of the mechanisms for resolving these conflicts are described.

(1) *Bureaucratic-professional conflict*
Social work, together with teaching and nursing, is a semi-

profession (Etzioni, 1969). In comparison with that of doctors or lawyers the training of social workers is short and their right to withhold information about their clients is less established. The police, for example, tend to feel that social workers should be prepared to help them in their inquiry by giving them information about clients. There is, too, a less specialized body of knowledge among social workers. Social work still relies very heavily on psychology, psychiatry and sociology for much of its theoretical content. In terms of formal qualifications, a specialized degree course in social work is, at least in Britain, only a recent innovation. Thus, social workers are less than fully legitimated in their professional status within the bureaucratic organization. They are less able to establish their right to professional autonomy in the eyes of other members of the organization. This tends to highlight the underlying tension between organizational bureaucratization and the professionalization of social workers.

It would, however, be a mistake to imply that there is a high degree of consensus amongst social workers as to the level of autonomy appropriate to their professional position. Blau and Scott (1963) have described the very different attitudes of 'professional' and 'bureaucratic' groups of social workers. There are also differences in attitudes between social workers who are professionally trained and those who are not, although it is important to note that Blau and Scott found this difference less pronounced than they had expected. The tensions between bureaucratic and professional forms of organization are thus complicated through the lack of consensus within the social work professional community itself.

(2) *Statistical records as bureaucratic control*
Although social workers constantly stress the unquantifiable nature of much of their social work practice, the records and filing system of a bureaucratic organization

are heavily dependent upon statistical measures of organizational activity. 'Dehumanised lists of cold figures correspond to the abstract, impersonal criteria that govern bureaucratic activities' (Blau, 1963, p. 36). In describing the use of statistical records of performance in an employment agency in America, Blau has described the unanticipated effects of this form of bureaucratic control upon the service given to clients.

In this agency eight indices of the worker's performance, such as the number of clients interviewed, the number of clients placed in a job and so on, were collected each month. Although originally designed by supervisors to provide information as the basis for rectifying poor performance, the fact that a supervisor would learn how many clients had been interviewed induced the interviewers to work faster. The records became a control mechanism in themselves.

As an effective bureaucratic mechanism for facilitating hierarchical control the statistical records had several beneficial effects. Speed of work and relations between supervisors and interviewers both improved. Necessary changes were more rapidly implemented. Yet in terms of the service to clients there were also a number of dysfunctional consequences. Because the performance index was not perfectly related to the behaviour it sought to measure, it was possible to improve the performance statistic without improving client service. In a displacement of organizational goals workers sought to improve the measure of performance rather than the performance itself. For instance, in an attempt to increase the number of referrals, clients were sent to apply for quite unsuitable jobs. At other times workers concentrated on those cases which were most easily placed to the neglect of those which were more difficult.

This is a good example of our earlier comment, that, given the problem of demonstrating social work performance, there is a temptation to resort to the completion of bureaucratic requirements as evidence of professional conduct.

(3) *Modes of conflict resolution*

In the concept of 'therapeutic supervision' these conflicts are ameliorated somewhat. Although perhaps more generally true of America, even in Great Britain supervision well beyond the student level can be an accepted part of a career in social work. Indeed it is sometimes mentioned as a specific attraction in advertisements for vacant appointments. In therapeutic supervision the supervisor assumes that a junior social worker's non-conformity to agency requirements is a function of the junior's own unconscious which the supervisor alone understands.

While this is an apparently non-bureaucratic type of control it is in fact often used to enforce the administrative requirements of the bureaucratic organization, such as meeting reporting deadlines, while avoiding offence to the professional's own self-image. As Scott (1969) comments, 'The supervisor emphasises his role as educator rather than administrative superior and confirms his self-image of professional rather than bureaucrat' (p. 108). This technique masks some of the basic conflict which underlies the situation.

Overt conflict may also be avoided by the professional's mode of adapting to tasks which originate within the bureaucratic aspects of the organization (Scott, 1969). First, administrative tasks may be redefined in terms of professional practice. In this way legal requirements on the frequency of visits, for example, can be conceived of in terms of client service. Second, if this is not possible, then the ability to accept authority may be interpreted as an ability to accept the realities of the situation, a mark of disciplined professional behaviour. In this way previously frustrating bureaucratic tasks become a source of professional satisfaction. In the third mode, that of professional reconciliation, organizational rules which apparently harm clients are placed within the context of a theory in which they are justified in terms of client welfare. Scott quotes the example of mothers who are refused financial assistance until they have filed paternity suits against the fathers of their illegitimate children. This is justified in terms of the children's identity needs. Similarly, local government rules limiting payments to foster parents are sometimes justified by social workers in terms of a theory of foster parent motivation.

These modes of adapting to administrative rules, then, function within the organization to mask the basic conflicts which underlie the situation of the professional social worker in the bureaucratic organization.

Front line organization

In spite of the conflicts between professional autonomy and controls of bureaucratic organization, there remain many areas of the social services in which social workers operate as peripheral units of front line organization. As Donnison (1965) notes,

> Many social services call for a concentration of some of the most highly skilled staff in the 'front line' from which the provision of the service takes place. The providers need discretion to operate freely within a broadly defined professional and administrative framework. (p. 240)

Yet although 'front line' organization is congruent with the professional's own self-image, it may have some consequences unanticipated in initial policy declarations.

In two studies, one of the services of the National Assistance Board (now the Supplementary Benefits Commission) (Marsden, 1969) and one of the services to the long-term unemployed (Sinfield, 1968), researchers have described the effect of the front line nature of the social security organizations upon the quality of service to clients.

98

In pressurizing unmarried mothers to return to work, in assessing the liability of a man who is cohabiting with a woman, and in granting discretionary payments, officers of the (then) National Assistance Board were given important powers, officially described as 'discretionary'. The Board, for example, did not make payments to mothers who cohabited, but nowhere was cohabitation clearly defined. In particular, attitudes to sexual relations were never spelled out clearly. Officers had wide discretion in assessing both the meaning and fact of cohabitation.

Marsden reports that these discretionary powers led to discrimination against unmarried mothers, the use of illegal methods to establish the facts of cohabitation, and a low level of provision for 'exceptional needs grants' : all this in spite of efforts on the part of the Board to provide the officers with relevant training in human relations linked to their day-to-day practice. Without effective control, the officers' own values and the requirements of organizational efficiency were used as decision-making criteria in these areas of practice. 'This was possible organizationally,' Marsden concludes, 'because NAB Officers had what has been called a "front line structure" ' (p. 210).

In a comparative survey of the long-term unemployed Sinfield comments on the discretion given to employment officers to select clients in allocating vacancies in their area. Since the placing of highly skilled workers was regarded as more 'professional' work, those who depended least upon the employment agency were in fact offered a better service. Often too, in officers' eagerness to ensure future co-operation with employers by sending the 'best' applicant, clients were sent for jobs for which they were clearly over-qualified. Although nowhere laid down as a policy decision, the front line position of officers did give rise to a policy in action in which some groups derived less benefit from the service than others. 'Dorothy Smith's analysis of the power of those working in direct contact with the clients in large scale organizations,' Sinfield concludes, 'illustrates how central directives may fail to be implemented' (p. 84).

These services may be regarded by some as outside the mainstream of social work practice but they do highlight two particularly relevant points. First, the officers described occupied the same structural position within their organization as the majority of professional field social workers and it was this front line position which allowed the employment of their own criteria in interpreting agency policy. Second, and perhaps more important, the resulting deficiencies in client service remained undetected by the agencies themselves. Only independent research studies revealed the nature of the decision-making criteria that were actually being employed. Even if it is argued that officers with adequate training will employ internalized professional criteria in areas of discretion, in front line organizations it is very difficult to assess the empirical validity of this claim since accurate information on policy in practice is the monopoly of front line units. In social work organizations with a front line structure it has too easily been assumed that statements on agency policy by a senior social worker are always accurate descriptions of real social policy in action.

Total institution

Many of the organizations providing social services of residential care, for children, the handicapped, or the aged, have structural features in common with the total institution. As I have already mentioned these institutions have important features which tend to inhibit any initial hopes of rehabilitation.

One of the most comprehensive studies of this type of organization is a survey of residential institutions and homes for the aged in England and Wales by Peter Townsend (1962). In describing admission procedures, life in the institution, and the effects upon old people of living in residential homes, Townsend examines the process of institutionalization. Inmates who, given a small amount of support from the domiciliary social services, could live on their own, are in fact reduced to a position of total dependency on the residential institution. Although many residents hope that their stay will be only temporary, restored family relations and a return to a 'normal', if 'supported', life in the community at large becomes impossible.

> We found that they tend to experience loss of occupation, isolation from family, friends and community, difficulties in forming more than tenuous relationships with members of staff and other residents, loneliness, loss of privacy and identity and collapse of powers of self-determination. These experiences vary in severity from one type of home to another but seem to exist in some measure everywhere. (Townsend, 1964, p. 434)

There is a good deal of evidence to suggest that this 'loss of identity' is to a large extent due, not to previous social history or to the process of ageing, but to those characteristics of the organizational environment which Goffman has described in his ideal type.

Much of Townsend's evidence suggests that the majority of old people do not freely choose to enter residential institutions and that they do not want to stay there permanently. It is certainly rare for a prospective resident to be given a choice of home. There are very few old people who decide themselves to dispose of their own home and possessions and only rarely do they have any choice in the room that they will occupy in the residential home. There is very little opportunity for residents to assess whether or not they are in fact likely to enjoy institutional life. All this acts to deprive the individual of his own identity and produce these reactions of institutionalization that have been observed in children's homes and other types of total institutions.

Many critics of total institutions have focused upon the low standard of material provision. This over-emphasis on material standards is perhaps mistaken, for even in very comfortable surroundings,

> the chief problem in communal homes is that too often the residents are shorn of status and dignity and are prevented from performing many tasks for themselves and for others of which they are still capable. (Townsend, 1964, p. 435)

This points to a more fundamental dilemma. Even if we no longer use total institutions as 'dumping grounds for inmates' (and this is debatable), in our desire to define and isolate categories of persons with highly specialized types of social need we have created entirely inappropriate forms of organizational environment. It may be administratively convenient to categorize types of clients but it often hinders the provision of the services that they really require. Given that many residents of homes for the aged are not there of their own choice, and given that the structure of total institutions inevitably assigns to residents a dependency role, there are severe restrictions on the kind of social services that can be provided within this type of organization.

Conclusion

In this chapter the term 'social work organization' has been used to include both agencies of social service such as Children's Departments, Probation Departments and offices of the Supplementary Benefits Commission, as well as institutions for residential care, such as children's homes and residential homes for the aged. I have commented on the position of the professional social worker within the bureaucratic organization. Then, in examining the front line structure of social work agencies, and the total character of many residential institutions, I have described the effects the organizational structure may have upon the service offered to clients.

11
Voluntary organizations

The relation between voluntary bodies and statutory agencies has been discussed at length, yet very little attention has been devoted to the internal structure of these organizations. However, a prerequisite to much of the debate is an understanding of these internal structures. For example, with the establishment by the government of a Young Volunteer Force Foundation, it is now generally accepted that voluntary organizations have an established role in the personal social services, but if a national policy on the use of volunteers in social work is to be implemented effectively at the local level the nature of the internal control structure of voluntary organizations must be examined. Wide variation both in the scope and level of activity of different branches of the same organization suggests that many voluntary bodies have only weak hierarchies of control when compared with the organization of the statutory bodies.

In this section, then, I first examine the process of formalization in voluntary organizations, second, the typically unstable nature of the goals of voluntary organizations, third, the way in which accounts of the organization may conflict within its permeable structure, and finally, possible patterns of control in front line voluntary organizations. In this way I hope to document the point, at least in respect to the use of voluntary organizations in the social services, that I made in the Introduction: that studies of internal organizational structure are a prerequisite to social policy formation.

Two further points should be made by way of introduction. First, there are, of course, many voluntary workers who are not part of any organization. By considering formally organized activity, I do not mean to imply that self-help movements, spontaneous neighbourhood groups or foster parents are insignificant. For any detailed account they are simply outside the scope of this book. Second, 'voluntary organization' is a very vague term and, while I want to avoid any definitional debate (as I have done throughout the book) it needs minimal clarification. The term has generally been used by sociologists to refer to those organizations which have very little capacity to discipline their participants. So this section will deal with that loose grouping of organizations which are concerned to use the efforts of voluntary workers in the provision of social and community services. Examples are International Voluntary Service, Women's Voluntary Service, Task Force, Service 9, Community Service Volunteers. They may employ a small number of full-time staff, but those organizations, such as councils of social service, which employ a full professional staff, financed from voluntary sources, are specifically excluded for consideration here.

Bureaucracy

As organizations which lack any formal capacity to control their members, precisely because they are 'volunteers', voluntary associations appear to be the least bureaucratic of all organizational forms. Yet over time a process of gradual formalization has been observed. The organization develops more rigid structures and becomes, in the end, detached from its ordinary membership base. In describing formalization as,

> an increasing complexity in the social structure, a progressive prescription and standardisation of social relationships and an increased bureaucratisation of the organisation (Chapin and Tsouderos, 1956, p. 306).

Chapin and Tsouderos detected a growth pattern, in a study of ten American voluntary organizations, which seems to be general. From the initial informal stage, a membership division of labour, executive and staff functions emerges. Eventually a distinct administrative body develops, membership groups appoint delegates for purposes of representation, standing committees are set up and there are problems of communication.

The organization creates more and more rules and procedures to conduct its business. The executive becomes detached from the everyday life of the organization. There are constant attempts to solve the communication problem. And, most important of all, the rank and file membership becomes increasingly passive and removed from the main areas of decision-making. Since voluntary organizations depend for their strength upon the commitment of their members, this last is the most serious of the unanticipated consequences of an approach to the bureaucratic model.

Goals

A major defect of the orthodox model, as I argued in Chapter 1, is the fact that it takes no account of changes in organizational goals, whether by succession or displacement. Both are features of voluntary organizations, but at the present state of research, generalizations in full answer to Blau's question 'What determines whether displacement of goals or succession of goals predominates in an organisation?' (1956, p. 95) are not possible. As the following case studies reveal, very different processes have been observed.

(1) *The Young Men's Christian Association*

Starting as an evangelical association for young men, the Y.M.C.A. has become a general leisure-time and character-development organization. It has shown a remarkable ability to adapt to differing community needs and has encompassed members well outside the scope of its initial objectives. In short, the Y.M.C.A. has successfully transformed from an evangelistic social movement to a general service organization (Zald and Denton, 1963).

This change has been accounted for, first in terms of the organization's 'enrolement economy'. It is immediately sensitive to demands for a changed service. Second, members of staff have only a poorly developed professional ideology and as Zald and Denton comment 'the more ideologically committed the professional to the means he uses the more difficult it will be to change the organization in which he operates'. Third, the initial goals and rules were only broadly defined allowing for many types of programmes within the organization. Finally, the decentralized and relatively autonomous centres of decision-making of the federated structure allow for more rapid adaptation to environmental changes.

(2) *The Women's Christian Temperance Union*

The W.C.T.U. faced a major environmental change at the abolition of prohibition (Gusfield, 1955). Humanitarian reform was initially a central theme of its doctrine and it conducted a welfare programme which was essentially maternalistic. From a middle-class position it sought to 'raise' the lower classes to its own cultural standards. After prohibition, however, its leaders were increasingly recruited from the lower socio-economic groups. Its doctrine became an expression of indignation directed at middle-class groups.

Thus, although in the face of environmental change the W.C.T.U. has not abandoned its formal goal of establishing temperance norms, it is no longer a middle-class organization devoted to dissuading working-class people from drinking and to improving their general welfare. The composition of its membership has changed and its attention has shifted to a new audience. It is now a working-class organization devoted to the discouragement of middle-class drinking. Much of its activity is limited to what Gusfield terms as indulgence in moral indignation.

(3) *The Townsend organization*
Based upon the plan by a Doctor F. E. Townsend in 1933 to give all United States citizens a retirement pension at 60, the goals of this organization became redundant at the passing of the Social Security Act in 1935 (Messinger, 1955). By 1951 membership had dropped by 97%. Patterns of activity changed drastically. In particular, initial fund-raising efforts became major trading ventures in themselves and the membership meetings gradually became purely social events. Thus this organization survived at all, not by changing its membership or goals, but by abandoning the initial goal and concentrating its attention almost entirely upon maintaining the organizational structure.

Each of these voluntary organizations, initially devoted to a service or welfare goal, adopted a different strategy in coping with a changed environment. However, the one overall finding that does emerge is that dissolution is a relatively rare phenomenon. The ability of an organization to extend, modify or displace its goals is an important factor in the process of organizational persistence.

Permeable organization

We have seen then that voluntary organizations tend to be particularly susceptible to the pressures of their social environment. Membership may drop or existing members may lose interest. A voluntary organization may lose its sources of financial support. It may be heavily criticized by government bodies or other agencies and organizations. At all points external social networks permeate the barriers of voluntary organizations. In short, they are permeable organizations.

A permeable structure has, as I have mentioned (Chapter 6), important effects upon the way in which different 'accounts' of the organization are managed. A voluntary organization has relatively few formal resources to control those who dissent from within, yet there are likely to be differences of opinion, for different groups of members are influenced by different social groups outside the organization. For example, senior members of staff are most open to the suggestion of government bodies, while members of local groups are more subject to local community pressures. Again two studies are used here to show how, in voluntary service organizations, different members may have very different pictures of the structure and purposes of the organization.

(1) *The National Foundation for Infantile Paralysis: two perceptions of structure*

The formal structure of the Foundation for Infantile Paralysis is that of a corporate type and we might expect the majority of voluntary members to perceive it in this way. However, while many did perceive it as a national organization, equally many saw it as a federation of local branches serviced by a national office (Sills, 1957). Those who saw the organization essentially as a national body regarded the local groups as branches of the national headquarters. They looked for leadership to the headquarters personnel and saw themselves as responsible to them. In contrast to this centralized view, many volunteers saw the Foundation as a number of loosely affiliated local branches. Directions from headquarters were regarded as encroachments upon the jurisdiction of the local organizations. Although the centralized service functions, such as producing campaign publicity, were well respected, the relation between branch organization and national office was not seen as one of hierarchical control.

Sills concludes that although the Foundation formally had a corporate type structure,

> The fact that nearly half of all volunteers actually perceive the Foundation as having a federation type structure is an important reason underlying volunteer interest and participation. As far as these Volunteers are concerned, the Foundation *has* a democratic structure. (p. 219)

(2) *A British voluntary service organization: three perceptions of structure*

In studying one British voluntary service organization three clearly separate views of the organization were apparent. Staff tended to see the organization in terms of a managerial model. The staff group itself was seen as the major locus of initiative and it was the task of local groups in the corporate structure to implement national policy. The goals of the organization were framed in national and international terms. Voluntary members of the central committees shared this centralized view but saw themselves, as representatives of the membership, as the major locus of initiative. It was the task of the staff to implement democratically formulated policy. Ordinary members of local groups, on the other hand, tended to view the structure as that of a federation. The local branch or group was seen as the main locus of organizational initiative and the tasks of both staff and national committees were seen as the provision of those services which were beyond the scope of the individual group. Here the goals of the organization were framed in terms of local community service.

The formal goals of the organization are stated in only very general terms and each group is thus able to legitimate its position by reference to some aspect of this statement.

Again it would be premature to generalize from a limited number of case studies. These data suggest, however, that not only different perceptions of the organization's goal, but also different perceptions of the formal structure itself, are sources of potential conflict in voluntary service organizations.

Front line organization

Whether the leaders are full-time members of staff or voluntary members of central and executive committees, voluntary service organizations present acute leadership problems. First, as we have seen, there can be a number of differing perceptions of the organization. Voluntary organizations are also characterized by the absence of any formal authority structure. Finally, many voluntary organizations are front-line organizations. The locus of much initiative rests with the individual volunteer or the local group. Individuals and volunteers often perform their work quite independent of other units and there are invariably major obstacles to any form of supervision. Thus we might expect leaders to resolve this dilemma by employing controls that are independent of the formal structure in a voluntary service organization.

In International Voluntary Service the communication structure is particularly important in this way (Smith, 1970). Central units can limit general access to certain types of information. On the other hand they are able, if they choose, widely to distribute particular information. By inviting outside speakers to meetings and by controlling the production of working papers and information sheets, central units can, too, create particular types of information for distribution in the organization.

In other voluntary organizations charismatic leadership may be important. Central units may also control the operative policy of the organization by recruiting only from particular groups of people. With increased attention being given to the training of volunteers this too, as in professional organizations, will be an important source of control through the internalization of certain normative standards.

These then are just some of the ways in which voluntary service organizations resolve the leadership dilemma.

Conclusion

This section has focused on the unstable nature of many voluntary organizations. They are subject to the process of formalization and in this and other ways their goals are subject to displacement and succession. Their permeable nature gives rise to divergent accounts of the organization and their front line nature gives rise to a leadership dilemma, and patterns of control that are independent of the organization's formal structure.

Suggestions for further reading

A great deal of the literature in the sociology of organizations is relevant to the needs of social workers. Much of it, however, is relevant indirectly, so the social worker who seeks to employ the findings of this field must be prepared to 'draw out' some of the relevance of the work for himself. This introductory book will have been successful if the reader feels that attempting the task is likely to prove worthwhile.

'Text books' and readers

Students often demand to know the single 'best buy' and it is tempting to recommend one. It would, however, be misleading to pretend that there is one single text book in this field. Blau and Scott's *Formal Organisations* (1963) is sometimes used in this way but I have already criticized the basic scheme employed (see Introduction). It does include a good deal that is relevant to professional practice. The best compact introduction is Etzioni's *Modern Organisations* (1964). This should be supplemented by the selective use of books of readings. Etzioni's *A Sociological Reader on Complex Organisations* (be sure to use the second and enlarged edition) (1969a) is excellent. His *Readings on Modern Organisations* (1969) contains some less well known contributions. The mammoth *Hand-*

book of Organisations (1965) edited by J. G. March attempts to cover the whole field. It has important contributions on some 'Specific Institutions'. Most social workers will wish to avoid the more theoretical chapters. The *Reader in Bureaucracy* (1952) edited by Merton and others is the standard reader on this aspect of the subject. *Behavioural Science for Social Workers* (1967) edited by Edwin J. Thomas contains a section of five articles on 'Organisational Factors in Service Agencies'. In all of these readers, intelligent browsing can yield high dividends.

History of the subject

In tackling new ideas it can often be a distinct advantage to understand the historical development of the subject. Nicos Mouzelis's, *Organisation and Bureaucracy* (1967) is neatly arranged. Specialists in the history of ideas find it dangerously over-simplified in parts.

'Classic' studies

A number of classic studies are widely quoted for significant developments which extend well beyond their empirical fields. These include Selznick, *T.V.A. and the Grass Roots* (1966, Lipset, Trow and Coleman, *Union Democracy* (1956), and in the field of industrial organization, Burns and Stalker, *The Management of Innovation* (1961), Dalton, *Men Who Manage* (1959), Gouldner, *Patterns of Industrial Bureaucracy* (1954) and Woodward, *Industrial Organisation: Theory and Practice* (1965). Of direct relevance to social work is Blau's *The Dynamics of Bureaucracy* (1956) and Sill's *The Volunteers* (1957).

Journals

Most sociologists who are engaged in research on welfare and social service organizations tend to publish in sociology rather than social work journals. Of the major British journals *The British Journal of Sociology*, *Sociology*, and *The Sociological Review* contain relevant articles from time to time. The *Administrative Science Quarterly* should also be mentioned. For 'addicts only' *Sociological Abstracts* present a brief summary and full references, for all relevant articles. Look under the headings 'Complex Organization (Management)' and 'Social Problems and Social Welfare'.

Bibliographies

Apart from the list at the end of this book, bibliographies and further references can be found in the majority of texts already mentioned. By far the most useful bibliography, however, is that of Blau and Scott's *Formal Organisations* (1963). The 800 or so items are classified under three headings, 'Type of Study', 'Type of Organization', and 'Major Topic'. This allows for very specific selection.

One particular suggestion

Numerous studies have been cited throughout the text of this book and it may be invidious to select just one of these for particular attention. As a final comment, however, I think that social workers will find Etzioni's *The Semi-Professions and their Organisation: Teachers, Nurses and Social Workers* (1969) particularly interesting.

Bibliography

ALBROW, MARTIN (1968) 'The Study of Organisations—Objectivity or Bias?' in Gould, J., *Penguin Social Science Survey*, Harmondsworth: Penguin Books.

AUBERT, VILHELM (1968) *Elements of Sociology*, London: Heinemann Educational Books Ltd.

(AVES) (1969) *The Voluntary Worker in the Social Services.* Report of a Committee jointly set up by the National Council of Social Service and the National Institute for Social Work Training under the Chairmanship of Geraldine M. Aves, C.B.E. London: The Bedford Square Press of the N.C.S.S. and George Allen & Unwin Ltd.

BARTON, RUSSELL (1966) *Institutional Neurosis*, Bristol: John Wright and Sons Ltd.

BECKER, HOWARD S. (1961) 'The Teacher in the Authority System of the Public School', in Etzioni, Amitai (Ed.) *A Sociological Reader on Complex Organisations*, New York: Holt, Rinehart and Winston.

BECKER, HOWARD S. (1963) *Outsiders: Studies in the Sociology of Deviance*, Glencoe, Ill.: The Free Press of Glencoe.

BELKNAP, I. (1956) *Human Problems of a State Mental Hospital*, New York: McGraw-Hill.

BERK, BERNARD, B. (1966) 'Organizational Goals and Inmate Organization' *American Journal of Sociology*, Vol. 71. pp. 522-34.

BIDWELL, CHARLES E. (1965) 'The School as a Formal Organization' in March, James G. (Ed.) *Handbook of Organizations*, Chicago: Rand McNally & Co.

BLAU, PETER M. (1956) *Bureaucracy in Modern Society*, New York: Random House.

BLAU, PETER M. (1963) *The Dynamics of Bureaucracy*, Chicago: The University of Chicago Press.

BLAU, PETER M. and SCOTT, W. R. (1963) *Formal Organizations. A Comparative Approach*, London: Routledge & Kegan Paul.

BURNS, TOM and STALKER, G. M. (1961) *The Management of Innovation*, London: Social Science Paperbacks.

CHAPIN, STUART F. and TSOUDEROS, JOHN E. (1956) 'Formalization Observed in Ten Voluntary Associations: Concepts, Morphology, Process', *Social Forces*, Vol. 34, pp. 306-9.

CICOUREL, AARON V. and KITSUSE, JOHN I. (1963) *The Educational Decision Makers*, Indianapolis: The Bobbs-Merrill Co. Inc.

CLEMMER, DONALD (1958) *The Prison Community*, New York: Holt, Rinehart and Winston. (First published 1940.)

CLARK, BURTON R. (1956) 'Organizational Adaptation and Precarious Values: A Case Study', *American Sociological Review*, Vol. 21, pp. 327-36.

CLOWARD, RICHARD A. (1960) 'Social Control in the prison' in Cloward, R. A. (*et al.*) *Theoretical Studies in Social Organization of the Prison*, New York: Social Science Research Council.

COHEN, GERDA L. (1964) *What's Wrong with Hospitals?* Harmondsworth: Penguin Books.

COLEMAN, JAMES S. (1961) *The Adolescent Society*, New York: The Free Press.

CRESSEY, DONALD R. (1965) 'Prison Organizations' in March, James G. (Ed.) *Handbook of Organizations*, Chicago: Rand McNally & Co.

CALTON, MELVILLE (1959) *Men Who Manage*, New York: John Wiley & Sons Inc.

DONNISON, D. V. and CHAPMAN, VALERIE (*et al.*) (1965) *Social Policy and Administration*, London: George Allen & Unwin Ltd.

EISENSTADT, S. N. (1958) 'Bureaucracy and Bureaucratization', *Current Sociology*, Vol. 7, No. 2, 1958.

ETZIONI, AMITAI (1960) 'Two Approaches to Organizational Analysis: A Critique and a Suggestion', *Administrative Science Quarterly*, Vol. 5, pp. 257-78.

ETZIONI, AMITAI (1961) *A Comparative Analysis of Complex Organizations*, New York: The Free Press.

ETZIONI, AMITAI (1964) *Modern Organizations*, Englewood Cliffs, New Jersey: Prentice-Hall Inc.

ETZIONI, AMITAI (1965) 'Organizational Control Structure' in March, J. G. (Ed.) *Handbook of Organizations*, Chicago: Rand McNally & Co.

ETZIONI, AMITAI (1969) *The Semi-Professions and their Organization: Teachers, Nurses, Social Workers*, New York: The Free Press.

ETZIONI, AMITAI (1969 a) *A Sociological Reader on Complex Organizations*, New York: Holt, Rinehart & Winston.

EYDEN, JOAN L. M. (1969) *Social Policy in Action*, London: Routledge & Kegan Paul.

GERTH, HANS H. and MILLS, C. WRIGHT (1948) (Trans. and Ed.) *From Max Weber: Essays in Sociology*, London: Routledge & Kegan Paul.

GIALLOMBARDO, ROSE (1966) *Society of Women: A Study of a Women's Prison*, New York: John Wiley & Sons, Inc.

GOFFMAN, ERVING (1961) *Asylums*, New York: Anchor Books, Doubleday & Co.

GOSS, MARY E. W. (1963) 'Patterns of Bureaucracy among Hospital Staff Physicians' in Friedson, E. (Ed.) *The Hospital in Modern Society*, New York: The Free Press.

GOULDNER, ALVIN W. (1954) *Patterns of Industrial Bureaucracy*, New York: The Free Press.

GOULDNER, ALVIN W. (1959) 'Organizational Analysis' in

Merton, Robert K. (*et al.*) (Eds.) *Sociology Today*, New York: Harper and Row.

GOULDNER, ALVIN W. (1961) 'Metaphysical Pathos and the Theory of Bureaucracy' in Etzioni, Amitai (Ed.) *A Sociological Reader on Complex Organisations.*

GROSS, NEAL; MASON, WARD S.; MCEACHERN, ALEXANDER W. (1958) *Explorations in Role Analysis*, New York: John Wiley & Sons, Inc.

GUSFIELD, JOSEPH R. (1955) 'Social Structure and Moral Reform: A Case Study of the Women's Christian Temperance Union', *American Journal of Sociology*, Vol. 66, pp. 221-32.

HALL, R. H. 'Bureaucracy and Small Organizations' *Sociology and Social Research*, Vol. 48, pp. 38-46.

HARRISON, PAUL M. (1959) *Authority and Power in the Free Church Tradition*, Princeton, New Jersey: Princeton University Press.

HODGSON, GODFREY (1969) 'Lock 'em up and leave 'em', *The Sunday Times*, 23 Nov. 1969.

HOMANS, GEORGE, C. (1951) *The Human Group*, London: Routledge & Kegan Paul.

JOHNSTON, NORMAN; SAVITZ, LEONARD, WOLFGANG (1962) *The Sociology of Punishment and Correction*, New York: John Wiley & Sons, Inc.

KATZ, FRED E. (1969) 'Nurses' in Etzioni, Amitai (Ed.) *The Semi-Professions and their Organization: Teachers, Nurses, Social Workers*, New York: The Free Press.

KING, ROY D. and RAYNES, NORMA V. (1968) 'Patterns of Institutional Care for the Severely Subnormal' *American Journal of Mental Deficiency*, Vol. 72, pp. 100-9.

LEONARD, PETER (1966) *Sociology in Social Work*, London: Routledge & Kegan Paul.

LEVINSON, PERRY (1964) *Chronic Dependency: A Conceptual Analysis*, Research Working Paper No. 1, Welfare Administration, Research Division U.S. Department of Health, Education and Welfare.

LIPSET, SEYMOUR M., TROW, M. A., and COLEMAN, J. S.

(1956) *Union Democracy*, Glencoe, Ill.: The Free Press.

LITWAK, EUGENE, and MEYER, HENRY J. (1966) 'A Balance Theory of Co-ordination between Bureaucratic Organization and Community Primary Groups' *Administrative Science Quarterly*, Vol. 11, pp. 31-58.

LITWAK, EUGENE, and MEYER, HENRY J. (1968) 'The School and the Family: Linking Organizations and External Primary Groups' in Lazarsfeld, Paul F. (*et al.*) (Eds.) *The Uses of Sociology*, London: Weidenfeld and Nicolson.

LORTIE, DAN C. (1969) 'The Balance of Control and Autonomy in Elementary School Teaching' in Etzioni, Amitai (Ed.) *The Semi-Professions and their Organization: Teachers, Nurses, Social Workers.*

MARCH, JAMES G. (1965) *Handbook of Organizations*, Chicago: Rand McNally & Co.

MARCH, JAMES G. and SIMON, HERBERT A. (1968) *Organizations*, New York: John Wiley & Sons Inc.

MARSDEN, DENNIS (1969) *Mothers Alone, Poverty and the Fatherless Family*, London: Allen Lane, The Penguin Press.

MATHIESSON, THOMAS (1965) *The Defences of the Weak*, London: Tavistock Publications.

MCCLEARY, RICHARD H. (1961) 'Policy Change in Prison Management' in Etzioni, Amitai (1961) (Ed.) *A Sociological Reader on Complex Organisations*, New York: Holt, Rinehart & Winston.

MECHANIC, DAVID (1962) 'Sources of Power of Lower Participants in Complex Organizations', *Administrative Science Quarterly*, Vol. 7, pp. 349-64.

MERTON, ROBERT K. (1940) 'Bureaucratic Structure and Personality', *Social Forces*, Vol. 17, pp. 560-8.

MERTON, ROBERT K. (*et al.*) (Eds.) (1952) *Reader in Bureaucracy*, New York: The Free Press.

MERTON, ROBERT K. (1957) *Social Theory and Social Structure*, London: The Free Press of Glencoe, Collier-Macmillan Ltd.

MESSINGER, SHELDON L. (1955) 'Organizational Transformation: A Case Study of a Declining Social Movement', *American Sociological Review*, Vol. 20, pp. 3-10.

MEYER, HENRY J. (*et al.*) (1968) 'Social Work and Social Welfare' in Lazarsfeld, Paul F. (*et al.*) (Eds.) *The Uses of Sociology*, London: Weidenfeld and Nicolson.

MICHELS, ROBERT (1915) *Political Parties*, Glencoe, Ill.: Free Press. Page references to Eden and Cedar Paul (Trans.) (1962) Free Press Paperback Edition, New York: The Free Press.

MINISTRY OF HOUSING AND LOCAL GOVERNMENT (1968) *Grouped Flatlets for Old People: A Sociological Study*, London: H.M.S.O.

MORRIS, PAULINE (1969) *Put Away: A Sociological Study of Institutions for the Mentally Retarded*, London: Routledge & Kegan Paul.

MORRIS, TERENCE and PAULINE (1963) *Pentonville. A Sociological Study of an English Prison*, London: Routledge & Kegan Paul.

MOUZELIS, NICOS P. (1967) *Organisation and Bureaucracy*, London: Routledge & Kegan Paul.

MUSGRAVE, PETER (1968) *The School as an Organization*, London: Macmillan & Co. Ltd.

MUSGROVE, F. and TAYLOR, R. H. (1965) 'Teachers' and Parents' Conceptions of the Teacher's Role', *British Journal of Educational Psychology*, Vol. 35, No. 2.

NOKES, PETER (1967) *The Professional Task in Welfare Practice*, London: Routledge & Kegan Paul.

NORMAN, FRANK (1969) *Banana Boy*, London: Secker & Warburg.

PARSONS, TALCOTT (1947) (Ed.) *Max Weber; The Theory of Social and Economic Organization*, New York: The Free Press.

PARSONS, TALCOTT (1960) 'A Sociological Approach to the Theory of Organizations' in *Structure and Process in Modern Societies*, Glencoe, Ill.: The Free Press.

PEABODY, R. L. (1964) *Organizational Authority*, New York and London: Atherton Press.

PERROW, CHARLES (1961) 'The Analysis of Goals in Complex Organizations', *American Sociological Review*, Vol. 26, pp. 854-66.

PERROW, CHARLES (1961a) 'Organizational Prestige: Some Functions and Dysfunctions', *American Journal of Sociology*, Vol. 66, pp. 335-41.

PERROW, CHARLES (1963) 'Goals and Power Structures— a Historical Case Study' in Freidson, E. (Ed.) *The Hospital in Modern Society*, New York: Free Press.

PERROW, CHARLES (1965) 'Hospitals: Technology, Structure, and Goals' in March, James G. (Ed.) *Handbook of Organizations*, Chicago: Rand McNally & Co.

REISS, ALBERT J. and BORDUA, DAVID J. (1967) 'Environment and Organization: A Perspective on the Police' in Bordua, David J. (Ed.) *The Police: Six Sociological Essays*, New York: John Wiley & Sons Inc.

RHENMAN, ERIC (1968) 'Organizational Goals', *Acta Sociologica*, Vol. 10, p. 275.

RICE, A. K. (1963) *The Enterprise and its Environment*, London: Tavistock Publications.

SCHEFF, THOMAS J. (1968) 'Negotiating Reality: Notes on Power in the Assessment of Responsibility', *Social Problems*, Vol. 16, pp. 3-17.

SCHRAG, CLARANCE (1954) 'Leadership Among Prison Inmates', *American Sociological Review*, Vol. 19, pp. 37-42.

SCOTT, W. RICHARD (1969) 'Professional Employees in a Bureaucratic Structure: Social Work' in Etzioni, Amitai (Ed.) *The Semi-Professions and their Organization: Teachers, Nurses, Social Workers*, New York: The Free Press.

(SEEBOHM) (1968) *Report of the Committee on Local Authority and Allied Personal Social Services*, Cmnd. 3703, London: H.M.S.O.

SELZNICK, PHILIP (1966) *T.V.A. and the Grass Roots*, Harper

Torchbook edition, New York: Harper and Row.

SHIPMAN, M. D. (1968) *Sociology of the School,* London: Longmans Green & Co. Ltd.

SILLS, DAVID L. (1957) *The Volunteers,* Glencoe, Ill.: The Free Press.

SINFIELD, ADRIAN (1968) *The Long-Term Unemployed,* Paris: Organization for Economic Co-operation and Development.

SINFIELD, ADRIAN (1969) *Which Way Social Work?* London: Fabian Tract 393.

SMITH, DOROTHY (1965) 'Front Line Organization of the State Mental Hospital', *Administrative Science Quarterly,* Vol. 10, pp. 381-99.

SMITH, GILBERT (1970) 'Control in a Voluntary Organisation', *Social Work (G.B.),* April 1970 (In press).

SMITH, HARVEY L. (1958) 'Two Lines of Authority: the Hospital's Dilemma' in Jaco, E.G. (Ed.) *Patients, Physicians and Illness: Source Book in Behavioural Science and Medicine,* Glencoe, Ill.: The Free Press.

STANTON, ALFRED H. and SCHWARTZ, MORRIS S. (1954) *The Mental Hospital,* New York: Basic Books.

SUGARMAN, B. (1967) 'Involvement in Youth Culture, Academic Achievement and Conformity in School: an Empirical Study of London Schoolboys', *British Journal of Sociology,* Vol. 18, No. 2.

SYKES, GRESHAM (1958) *Society of Captives,* Princeton: Princeton University Press.

SYKES, GRESHAM (1961) 'The Corruption of Authority and Rehabilitation' in Etzioni, Amitai (Ed.) *Complex Organizations: A Sociological Reader,* pp. 191-197, New York: Holt, Rinehart & Winston.

THOMAS, EDWIN J. (Ed.) (1967) *Behavioural Science for Social Workers,* New York: The Free Press.

THOMPSON, J. D. and MCEWEN, W. J. (1958) 'Organizational Goals and Environment: Goal Setting as an Interaction Process', *American Sociological Review,* Vol. 23, pp. 23-31.

THOMPSON, VICTOR A. (1961) *Modern Organizations*, New York.

TOWNSEND, PETER (1962) *The Last Refuge*, London: Routledge & Kegan Paul. Page references to abridged edition (1964).

WAREHAM, JOYCE (1967) *An Introduction to Administration for Social Workers*, London: Routledge & Kegan Paul.

WESSEN, ALBERT F. (1958) 'Hospital Ideology and Communication between Ward Personnel' in Jaco, E. G. (Ed.) *Patients, Physicians and Illness: Source Book in Behavioural Science and Medicine*, Glencoe, Ill.: The Free Press.

WOODWARD, JOAN (1965) *Industrial Organization: Theory and Practice*, London: Oxford University Press.

ZALD, MAYER N. and DENTON, PATRICIA (1963) 'From Evangelism to General Service: The Transformation of the Y.M.C.A.', *Administrative Science Quarterly*, Vol. 8, pp. 214-34.

ZALEZNIK, ABRAHAM and JARDIM, A. (1968) 'Management' in Lazarsfeld, P. F. (*et al.*) (Eds.) *The Uses of Sociology*, London: Weidenfeld and Nicolson.

DATE DUE